Be the Meatball

Custom Résumés to Stand Out
from the Crowd and Get the Interviews You Deserve©

By Bestselling Author
Don Burrows

Companion Text to Online Course
BE THE MEATBALL: Top Candidate Custom Résumés To Win Interviews and Stop Being Ignored for Promotions You've Earned

TopCandidateResumes.com

Disclaimer

This book is intended as a personal development tool to offer promotion-seekers, (passed over for promotions they know they've earned,) or jobseekers, (ignored for work they've proven they can do,) an Inner Game and résumé system to win interviews by customizing their relevant professional accomplishments and skills to the specific requirements of each opportunity they seek, thus presenting themselves as TOP CANDIDATES each time they apply.

Done correctly, their custom credentials will STAND OUT from their competition, like a MEATBALL on a plate of spaghetti.

This book is based on the author's 35+ years of professional Human Resources experience. The fact that **The BE THE MEATBALL Custom Résumé System©** has worked for others is not a guarantee that it will work for everyone. Therefore, because of the almost infinite number of variables beyond the author's knowledge or control, the reader is advised to consult with open-minded professional HR or job search advisors of his or her choice regarding the use of the information contained herein.

The author has empirical proof that his custom résumé system works for those who will work the system as designed. He has done his best to create a factually accurate D-I-Y custom résumé creation book. Neither the author nor publisher assume any responsibility for errors or omissions, and specifically disclaim any liability resulting from the use or application of information contained herein.

Be the Meatball. Custom Résumés to Stand Out from the Crowd and Get the Interviews You Deserve©

Cover Design: BookClaw.com

As the purchaser, this book is licensed for your use only. If you wish to share the contents with others, please purchase as many copies as necessary for them. If you are reading this book and did not purchase it yourself or receive it as a gift purchased for you, it would be ethical of you to return it and purchase your own copy. This is how the author makes his living, and he thanks you for honoring that fact as well as the time, thought and energy he put into creating it. Please be ethical and refuse to participate in or encourage others to engage in piracy of copyrighted materials. What would your mother say?

ISBN: 978-0-578-60881-5

Dedication

First and foremost - to Karin Burrows … Thank you for giving me the time to make this happen – for us

To Eric Castaneda … Thank you for the twin concepts of *Generic 90%ers* and *Motivated 10%ers*

To Crystal Young … Thank you for adding *"finding joy"* to *"most proud"* as a new criterion to identify meaningful accomplishments

To Karen Druliner . . . Thank you for editing of the first manuscript

To Jeanine Blackwell of JeanineBlackwell.com . . . Thank you for guiding my course from dream to idea to reality

To Scott Bell . . . Thank you for you video critiquing and editing

To Chris Burrows of GreenLightWebSolutions.com . . . Thank you for developing my website

To Rachel Braynin . . . Thank you for birthing this Lulu of a book

And, to single moms and women primary breadwinners everywhere, passed over for promotions you know you've earned … Let's stop making it so easy for them to ignore you.

My Personal Note to You

You may be asking yourself why you'd need a résumé when applying for a promotion?

"I mean, really? Why? I work at the company and they know me. Right?"

Decision-makers know what they know about you, but do they know all *you* want them to know about why *you're* perfect for the promotion?

If you're a single mom, the sole provider for your children, tired of being invisible, ignored, stressed out, and passed over for promotions you know you've earned, it's time to STAND OUT and present yourself as the TOP CANDIDATE for the promotion. I like the image of a MEATBALL on top of a plate of blend-in spaghetti.

Decision-makers can select from two groups of applicants. Group 1 are the few who have gone to the effort to make themselves TOP CANDIDATES for the promotion. Group 2 are the *"spaghetti applicants©,"* folks whose generic, one-size-fits-all résumés give decision-makers no reason to interview them, so they don't.

Especially when not a requirement for consideration, a custom résumé and targeted cover letter, based on the specific requirements of the promotion sought, demonstrate personal initiative and make you memorable as an immediate stand-out candidate. Decision-makers do not ignore TOP CANDIDATES.

That same logic applies if you are seeking a promotion to a new job away from your current employer.

Want the Interview? Be the Meatball, not the spaghetti. ©

Table of Contents

Preface

"Judge by Results. Often Harsh. Always Fair."
- Attributed to Brian Klemmer, 1950 - 2011

Your Transformation from PASSED OVER and IGNORED to TOP CANDIDATE Starts Now

The BE THE MEATBALL Custom Résumé System©

TWO QUESTIONS:

What's Your Biggest Fear about Being Passed Over for Promotions You Know You've Earned?

In today's uncertain political and economic climate, and with serious talk of a possible 2020 recession, if you're:

- A single mom and the primary provider for your family, and
- An employed, high-5-figure, mid-career professional, ignored for promotions you know you've earned . . .

Your biggest fear is for your family.

If there's a recession in 2020 and you lose your job, how quickly will your résumé win you interviews so you can get hired and back to work?

This book, and the online course it supports, *(BE THE MEATBALL – Top Candidate Custom Résumés to Win Interviews and Stop Being Ignored for Promotions You've Earned,)* will help protect your family.

Note: Before you begin doing the work in Chapter 1, I recommend you read, or at least skim, the entire book so you have an idea of the flow of the process and can begin to make some time estimates to complete the book.

Answers to Two Essential Questions

1. Is BE THE MEATBALL© right for me?

Yes, if you dare to undertake a personal transformation from Generic 90%er© (using the same generic résumé again and again, or no résumé at all) to Motivated 10%er© (creating custom résumés and targeted cover letters to be the TOP CANDIDATE for each promotion you seek).

Yes, if you're an employed, high-five-figure, mid-career professional, are tired of being passed over for promotions you know you've earned, or ignored for jobs you've proven you can do, and are willing to take action to jump-start your career.

Yes, if you want to stop following the Boilerplate Herd and reignite your career.

Yes, if you want to learn to create your own promotions or jobs, so you can bypass the competition.

Yes, if your Inner Game and your job search self-confidence are the pits, and you don't like yourself when you go "Victim" and blame others for your career problems.

Yes, if at your core you're a proactive person who is motivated to make and keep your commitments and you're willing to buck convention and try a transformative new system that will require commitment, spirit, time and energy, and when complete, will enable you to win interviews as the TOP CANDIDATE, whenever you want them.

And Yes, if you're ready to STAND OUT, like a Meatball, and stop blending in, like spaghetti.

But No, if you want another short-cut to another cookie-cutter, generic *"dates-and-duties" résumé.* Keep moving. We're not a good fit.

2. Has the BE THE MEATBALL custom résumé system© worked for others?

Oh, boy! Has it ever!

I've been refining this system for over 30 years. I've helped hundreds (of *promotion-seekers* passed over for promotions they knew they'd earned and *jobseekers*, ignored for work they had proven they could do,) use this system to grab decision-makers' attention, win interviews as top candidates, and get hired.

And for 18 of those years, in-house recruiting was an essential part of my domestic and international HR management career.

Please visit TopCandidateResumes.com/successes/, or click the link if you're reading this as an e-book, to read testimonials and see custom résumés of twelve mid-career professionals, who used my system to become top candidates, won interviews and were promoted or hired.

If you're the primary provider for your family and talk of a possible recession in 2020 makes you jumpy, and you're an employed, high-5-figure, mid-career professional, passed over for promotions you know you've earned, you need this book, now.

Here Are Six Reasons Why

1. Protect Your Family in Case of a Recession in 2020. If decision-makers ignore you because your current résumé gives them no reason to pay attention to you now, when the economy is OK, how quickly will it get you interviews if there's a recession and you get laid off? NOW is the time to proactively protect your career and your family, strengthen your job search self-confidence, recession-proof your résumé, and transform yourself from just another generic applicant hoping for an interview into a TOP CANDIDATE, able to win interviews when you want them.

2. Win interviews as the TOP CANDIDATE each time you apply. If you can't get the interview, your experience and education won't matter. And since your current résumé isn't working, stop using it. When you've learned to create custom résumés and cover letters based on the specific requirements of the promotion you seek, you'll be the top candidate, impossible for decision-makers to ignore.

3. Win Your "INNER GAME." It takes courage — job search self-confidence — to stop following the *Boilerplate Herd*, to stop using the traditional, two-page, reverse-chronological, *"dates-and-duties"* résumé *"they"* say you should use. Those generic résumés are nothing more than *"job search junk mail"*© and make it easy for decision-makers to ignore you. If your experience and education make you right for the job, your credentials, customized to the requirements of the promotion you seek, will give them powerful reasons to interview you, and ignore your competition.

4. Have a LIFETIME CAREER PLAN©. Part 1 of the course will enable you to win your Inner Game, so you'll have the job search self-confidence to be the TOP CANDIDATE, from now until you choose to retire. In Part 1, your final Inner Game exercise will be to create your custom *Lifetime Career Plan©* - your personal Inner Game blueprint - so you can always regain your job search self-confidence. It will become the foundation of your Inner Game. You can update it as needed and return to it throughout your career when you need to rebound and rebrand yourself and you need to be reminded why you're the top candidate.

5. Only seek promotions where and when you'll be the TOP CANDIDATE. Every time you talk yourself into applying for a promotion where you think/hope your experience lets you *"give it a shot,"* and decision-makers pass you over without even a finger twiddle, it's a gut slam to your Inner Game and your job search self-confidence. Stop doing that. Only apply where and when you can be the top candidate.

6. "BE THE MEATBALL, not the spaghetti"©. Decision-makers who ignored your generic credentials and passed you over for promotions before, won't anymore. With the TOP CANDIDATE custom résumés and targeted cover letters you'll create, you'll STAND OUT, like a meatball on a plate of forgettable fettuccini. Decision-makers will scramble to interview you.

Remember:

If your résumé doesn't give decision-makers good reasons to interview you, they won't.

INTRODUCTION TO PART 1

Winning Your "Inner Game"

Your "Inner Game"

If you're committed to following the *Boilerplate Herd* by using the traditional, generic, two-page, reverse-chronological, activities-based résumé that looks like everyone else's, and making it so easy for decision-makers to ignore you, please stop reading. Save your time, money and energy. I cannot help you.

HOWEVER, if it's more important to you to showcase your relevant professional accomplishments and skills than it is to make it possible for decision-makers to scan your credentials in 7 - 10 seconds, if you dare to create and use custom résumés and cover letters based on the specific requirements of the promotion you seek, this book and course are for you.

To win interviews for promotions or jobs... BE THE MEATBALL, NOT THE SPAGHETTI©

As we get into your Inner Game, my questions for you right now are:

- Will you commit to making this transformative journey a flowing experience, or will it be a grind?
- Will you go "Victim," quit on yourself, "settle" for mediocrity, and let your career stagnate?
- Will you continue to take well-intended but timid advice causing you to play a losing *"Inner Game,"* and blame your situation on everyone else?

Or, are you going to be "Response-Able."? Will you dare to identify and embrace the brilliance of your accomplishments, let the system rise to meet you, and be changed for the better?

The change is only as hard as you choose to make it. You get to decide how you are going to show up. You just need to decide. And if it would help to know more about me please visit TopCandidateResumes.com/About-Don for my résumé.

My Promise to You

Once you've completed this course and mastered "Be the Meatball©", you'll have won your Inner Game, be a TOP CANDIDATE, and decision-makers will no longer ignore you for interviews you know you've earned.

Here are the critical things I want you to think about as we begin:

1. Winning interviews for promotions by always being the top candidate is an acquirable, *transformational mindset.* You'll never again be satisfied being just another generic applicant whose generic résumé is *job search junk mail©* that blends in with all the other generic résumés of your competition.

2. BE THE MEATBALL© works at all levels - hourly, managerial, individual contributor, executive, returning military, or recent college graduate seeking first job.

3. However, it is not a magic bullet. It only works when you apply where it makes sense for you to apply - where your relevant professional accomplishments and your special skills and abilities will make you the TOP CANDIDATE.

4. It is not a fill-in-the-blanks cookie-cutter template. Reaping the benefits will require you to work, to think, and to devote time and energy.

5. It is not right for 90% of job/promotion seekers, the group I call *Generic 90%ers,©* who prefer template résumés, short-cuts, and quick fixes.

6. It is perfect for the group I call *Motivated 10%ers©* - the 10% of job/promotion-seekers who will commit to following the system, and then follow-through on their commitment.

7. BE THE MEATBALL© is a modular system based on building accomplishments and skills data banks containing information

you'll customize to the specific requirements of each opportunity you seek. You can make yourself the TOP CANDIDATE each time you apply.

8. You'll never *"update your résumé"* again because each résumé will be custom - an original.

Please read #s 7 and 8 again. I want to make sure you realize how unique and flexible your custom finished product will be.

If I have not scared you off, please go to TopCandidateResumes.com/successes, read the 12 testimonials and study the custom résumés and targeted cover letters you'll find there. Pretty soon, yours could be there as well.

They belong to 12 smart, competent people, just like you. They all took a courageous leap of faith and dared to STAND OUT and BE THE MEATBALL.

Some were fed up with being passed over or ignored for opportunities they knew should have been theirs. Others simply recognized a career-advancing tool when they saw it and enthusiastically embraced a new system.

By applying what you are about to learn, they either reignited their careers, or took them to the next level.

My Story: Why I've Earned the Right to Advise You

I don't believe we are here to mark time doing work that makes us unhappy, to *"settle,"* or be bored, or do purposeless work.

That drains the soul's energy.

I know it's devastating to be passed over for promotions you've earned, ignored for jobs you've proven you can do, or abruptly laid off from work you were good at and liked doing.

Your Inner Game — your self-esteem, your resiliency, and job search self-confidence — goes into tailspin, and unintentionally you go "Victim" and blame everything and everyone for your situation.

I know, because I've been there. Over 15 months, I:

1. Went through a painful and costly divorce where unknown to me, the judge and my ex were church buddies,

2. Laid off 90 employees, and was one of a handful transferred to corporate headquarters, 1,200 miles away from my children,

3. Was recruited to a new company, promoted and relocated back to within 50 miles of my kids. Seven months into that new job, I was getting my life back together when suddenly I was one of 130 people laid off after Corporate decided to shut my division.

4. Received outplacement from a national firm. Following their generic process for six months, I sent out over 300 résumés for work I had proven I could do. I went on three interviews and got no offers. After the third interview, the corporate VPHR told me I was qualified for the job I was interviewing for, but that he would not hire me. He said that if he did, the CEO would fire him and promote me into his job.

First the divorce, then the church buddies, then relocation, then new company and relocation back, then layoff, then followed generic advice and was ignored over 300 times, then the third VPHR's words . . .

At that point, my fear and mounting sense of *"Victim"* ignited like a white-hot flame.

My INNER GAME radiated toxicity.

In retrospect, I acknowledge I was responsible for managing my feelings, and I'm certain my frustration, anger, and *"victim-ness"* came through in the tone of my cover letters and what few phone interviews I got. As I fearfully watched my savings disappear, I was not a pleasant person.

I was responsible for prolonging my situation.

No wonder no one wanted to hire me.

Nobody wants to hire *"desperate."*

Yet out of that mess came self-awareness and this solution: I decided that if the third VPHR thought I was corporate VPHR material, then I should too. And in that transformative moment, one that reignited my job search self-confidence, my Inner Game went from pathetic and puny to potent and powerful.

I stopped using the *blend-in, dates-and-duties generic job search junk mail© cookie-cutter* résumé the outplacement people were pushing, and created a new accomplishments-based résumé containing only HR work I loved to do, and was good at doing (management and supervisory development training, recruiting, organization development, outplacement, restructuring, coaching and counselling, and conflict resolution - in Spanish as well as English).

That unconventional résumé was nothing less than a job description of my ideal job and was my first attempt to create a position for myself.

It worked.

In addition to creating a résumé that would **stand out**, I decided I would ignore HR and their recruiting *"cattle chute"* that most of the time ignored me.

Ignore HR's Recruiting "*Cattle Chutes,*" Where Qualified Applicants Send Their Résumés to Die

I decided I would **be bold**, ditch the *Boilerplate Herd,* and send my résumé directly to 100 CEOs.

I got all the contact information I needed from the *Puget Sound Business Journal's* **Book of Lists** (BizJournals.com).

My new résumé was four pages long. Rather than start in the traditional manner, it began with my Relevant Professional Accomplishments and the Special Skills and Abilities I used to achieve them.

My complete chronological work history, education, military and such were on the last page. My three-paragraph cover letter was attention-getting and contained an intriguing value proposition.

While I waited for responses from those 100 CEOs, I shared my new mindset, résumé, and cover letter with other ignored job seekers in the outplacement office. Several asked my help to redo their résumés.

As I began to get invitations to meet with CEOs, my Inner Game went from foul to fabulous. Rather than being impressed and happy for me, the outplacement company director was mad. (My skeptical mind suspected their business model was built on folks being ignored and unemployed for as long as possible.)

In all, twenty of those 100 C-Suite folks invited me to meet with them. Based on my accomplishments and skills and the problems he had that I could solve for him, a CEO created a position just for me. He relocated me from Delaware to Vancouver, WA at a lovely rate of pay.

Note: Please don't think you have to be a VP for my system to work for you. This strategy, TOP CANDIDATE mindset, and the job search self-confidence you'll gain will work at any level. You just need to work the system.

By transforming my mindset from generic applicant to TOP CANDIDATE, I won my Inner Game and had the job search self-confidence to stop sending generic job search junk mail©.

And, in the process I created a promotion and my next job.

Before you proceed, please study the custom résumés and cover letters you'll find on TopCandidateResumes.com/successes.

Be Bold! Leave The "Boilerplate Herd." Find A Need Going Unmet That You Can Fill, And Let Decision-Makers Know

By skipping the HR cattle chute and going directly to the C-Suite, I got back to work by creating a job doing only what I loved to do and was well-paid for doing it.

Three times over 18 years in Corporate America, I have created jobs or promotions for myself by *identifying needs going unmet*, and then presenting myself as the solution to those needs.

Was it quick and easy to do? No.

Did it work? Yes.

Will it work for you? If you're determined to remain a Generic 90%er©, I doubt it.

But if you're a Motivated 10%er©... Yes!

It has also worked for others whose Inner Games were weak at that moment but who, at their cores, were Motivated 10%ers©.

So, if you are a Generic 90%er© and your Inner Game is weak, you can commit to becoming a Motivated 10%er© and doing what it takes to win your Inner Game.

Or not. Like I said – you get to decide.

And if you're on the road to becoming a Motivated 10%er©, let's begin your transformation.

CHAPTER 1

Your "*Inner Game*" Determines the Success or Failure of Your Career

How much do you and the people depending on you for a roof over their heads and food on the table have invested in your career?

What are your financial obligations to them? Mortgage or rent? Alimony? Child support? Investments and savings for emergencies and retirement? College tuition? Vacations? Credit card debt? Cars?

Whatever the answer, in terms of time, money, energy, emotion, and your futures, it's a lot.

If your career has hit a wall, the obligations keep on, even if the money doesn't. You've got a lot to lose. But even more to gain.

Please don't lose sight of that last point, or your family, or the possibility of a 2020 recession, as you read this book.

Are you an employed, high-five-figure, mid-career professional facing any, or all, of these situations?

- Early in your career, promotions came easily, but no longer. Not only are promotions not there, the competition is getting tougher. And younger.
- Your peers and colleagues are getting promoted into jobs you think should be yours.
- You suspect you've gone about as far as you can go with your current company BUT think you're at an age when no one will want to hire you.
- Just thinking about starting over somewhere else makes you want to take a nap.

Any of these realities is justification enough for you to feel depressed. If you're dealing with several, or all, of them, it's no wonder your INNER GAME is the pits.

What's Your "Inner Game?"

Your Inner Game is how you see yourself. It's how you choose to present yourself when you apply for a promotion or a new job. It's the strength of your resiliency and your job search self-confidence, or lack thereof, when you're an employee or in the job market.

It's your spirit of optimism, or pessimism, your ability to win the next promotion so your career continues to progress as you want it to. It's your self-talk (the little voice inside you) that continually reinforces how great you are or tells you you're falling behind.

Chances are excellent that if promotions you know should be yours are going to others, you're losing your Inner Game.

In my 18 years of being an HR decision-maker, I never intentionally hired or promoted anyone who was playing a losing Inner Game. Just as you can sense when you need to stay away from someone because of a vibe they are throwing off, when you're playing a losing Inner Game, you're putting out that same *"stay away"* vibe that decision-makers and others pick up and react to. It's a downward cycle.

Do You Follow The "Boilerplate Herd"?

"Boilerplate Herders" do what everyone else does. They reuse the same traditional, generic, two-page, reverse-chronological, dates-and-duties résumé, because that's how "they" say it should be done. Those generic résumés *blendinlikestrandsofspaghettionaplate*. Decision-makers ignore them, and that's why I call generic résumés *"job search junk mail©."*

As a former in-house recruiter, I promise you, boilerplate résumés are ridiculously easy for decision-makers to ignore.

Said another way - Boilerplate Herders are responsible for their stalled careers.

Victim or Response-Able?

What keeps your career stuck? It's not the economy or politics; it's losing your Inner Game and seeing yourself as "Victim." Here's what I've witnessed, personally experienced, and believe to be a universal truth:

Playing a never-ending, losing INNER GAME, and putting out a continual stream of "Victim Vibes" of anger, fear, and resentment, keeps you stuck.

Being the *Top Candidate* Depends on Winning Your Inner Game

Why? It takes guts to stop following the Boilerplate Herd and stop mass-distributing *"spaghetti résumés."* When your Inner Game lets you decide to stop being the spaghetti and instead BE THE MEATBALL©, you'll win interviews as the top candidate. I promise.

Earlier I asked you to study the 12 résumés and success stories on my website. If you blew me off, it's that kind of Generic 90%er© behavior that keeps you stuck. Please study them now. Please pay particular attention to the credentials of Greg, E.C., Jen, Rachel, Gary, and Alejandro.

At the end of each person's Representative Professional Accomplishments section, you'll find a unique personal accomplishment statement. (Alejandro put his in an oval at the end of his résumé.)

It took courage for each of them to include their personal accomplishment statement. Doing so is an essential element in my system to make them a memorable Meatball, the person decision-makers eagerly looked forward to interviewing.

Personal accomplishments converted into *business accomplishment statements* catch the reader's interest and tell them a lot about the person's character and what traits and values they'll bring to a promotion or new job.

If you want to get a jump on the process, please begin thinking about the unique personal accomplishment you'll use to end your custom résumé.

Three Transformative Mindset Shifts You Must Make

Mindset Shift #1

"Take the first step in faith. You don't have to see the whole staircase, just take the first step." Dr. Martin Luther King, Jr.

I know my system works, but you don't. So, I'm going to ask you to take that first step in faith, believing that my system will help you get your career back on-track.

Stop following Boilerplate Herd Generic Advice like this:

1. Your résumé can't be more than two pages, because no one will read more than that.
2. You should only include jobs you think are relevant.
3. Your résumé must focus on your work history and be in reverse chronological order, starting with your most recent job and working backward, so it's easy for a screener to quickly skim it.
4. There's no need to present employment dates in month, year - just "year" is OK.
5. There's no need to explain gaps in employment in your résumé; you can explain them in the interview.
6. Your résumé should only go back ten years because anything older than that is too old to be of value.
7. You don't need an Objective Statement.
8. Decision-makers distrust accomplishments-based résumés because you can hide or omit stuff.
9. Cover letters are no longer needed.
10. Getting interviews is a numbers game, so you must apply whenever and wherever you think you have a shot.

Those ten points are fine if you are writing your résumé to make it easy for the screeners to screen you out, which means **you intend to continue being a Generic 90%er© - passed over and ignored.** However, continuing to use your generic job search junk mail© résumés will continue to make you invisible — just another strand of forgettable fettuccini.

If you want to become a Motivated 10%er© and win interviews as a TOP CANDIDATE for each promotion you seek, from now until you retire, you'll ignore those 10 points, and *Stop Committing "Job Search Suicide."* ©

Mindset Shift #2

"I have written eleven books, but each time I think, 'Uh oh, they're going to find out now. I've run a game on everybody, and they're going to find me out." Author Maya Angelou

This is called The Imposter Syndrome. It goes hand-in-hand with winning or losing your Inner Game. In my experience, "Victim" and "Imposter Syndrome" both result in job search suicide. ©

Sometimes, even when you know you're competent and you know your Inner Game is solid, sudden little flashes of self-doubt, or thoughts like, *"They'll never promote me. I'm too... [fill in the blank]"* can creep in, and you feel like a fake.

If the Imposter Syndrome catches you unaware and you let it worm its way into your newly developing top candidate mindset, you'll be sorry. This is a dangerous time for your new mindset. It's delicate, like a little spring flower that has just popped out of the soil. Fragile. One careless misstep and the flower is squished.

Similarly, one Imposter thought, left unchallenged and permitted to take root, can grow, canceling out all your progress and weakening the foundation of your new Motivated 10%er© mindset. Without even being aware of it, you could slide back into your old "Victim" mindset.

The only way I know to mitigate the Imposter Syndrome is to be constantly on guard. When you recognize it, refocus your attention on your Representative Professional Accomplishments and the Special Skills and Abilities you used to achieve them.

If you're proud of having achieved something, it is, by definition, an accomplishment.

Review your accomplishments periodically to reaffirm and remind yourself of your competency.
Begin to list them now, because later in the course, you're going to write essays about the accomplishments of which you are most proud or that brought you joy and analyze them to identify the skills you used to achieve them. Then you will convert some into Accomplishment Statements, and store in your Accomplishments Data Bank.

Then, when you've identified a promotion for which your accomplishments and skills will qualify you to be the TOP CANDIDATE, you'll dive into your Accomplishments and Skills Data Banks, select ONLY the ones that most precisely fit the requirements of the opportunity you seek, and customize them to the specific requirements of the promotion.

By presenting yourself as the TOP CANDIDATE, you'll banish the Imposter Syndrome and assure yourself of an interview.

And that, in a nutshell, is the essence of BE THE MEATBALL©. As you work through the process, you'll learn to authentically *"tastefully boast."*

The more comfortable you are with tastefully boasting, the more response-able you'll be. And to the degree that you strengthen your Inner Game, you'll decrease the power of the "Imposter Syndrome." It may never disappear entirely, but with continual vigilance, you can mitigate its impact on you and your career.

Mindset Shift #3

"When the why gets stronger, the how gets easier." Motivational speaker Jim Rohn

Your first question should never be, *"HOW will I get this promotion?"*

Your first question should always be *"WHY do I want this promotion?"*

If your first question is, *"HOW do I get this interview?"* and you can only think of one solution (maybe use your current generic résumé?) and you settle for that solution and start applying it without identifying and seriously considering others, you're at a distinct disadvantage. If it doesn't work, you're dead in the water.

So, take some time to ask yourself more effective questions, like:

- Do I want this promotion? And if so, why?"
- Longer term, where do I want my career to go, and why will this promotion help get me there?
- Suppose I look beyond my current job, identify needs going unmet here that the company does not see, and create both a new job and/or promotion for myself by being the solution to those needs?
- If I could add value to the company and bring work-joy to myself by restructuring my current job to include only the things I love to do and am good at doing, what would I leave in? What would I omit? What would I add? Why not give that a shot?

Those are all thoughtful, challenging questions that will lead you far beyond just applying for the generic, business-as-usual promotion that your competition also wants. The trick is to develop enough **Inner Game self-confidence** to look for needs going unmet, and then have enough **relevant accomplishments, skills** and **courage** to present yourself as the solution to those needs.

Do that and you'll create your unique opportunities, and completely sidestep the competition.

Am I Bending Your Brain Just A Little?

I hope so. Here are four more questions to prepare you for TOP CANDIDACY:

1. What's Unique About You?

I loved to ask that question when interviewing both promotion-seekers and job applicants, because how they reacted, and their responses told me a lot about them.

When the applicant gave me a boring, Generic 90%er© response that showed no prior thought, like, *"I'm good with people,"* it was Strike One.

But I was overjoyed when an applicant said something like, *"I've given that an awful lot of thought and these are the top three things I've identified: 1) Because I'm easy to talk to, people readily open up to me, so we can get to the real issues faster. 2) Because I value thoughtful responses in others, I make it a point to think before I speak. 3) People like to work for me because I share what I know and have launched more careers than any other manager in the company."*

Give thought to this question because if you give a vague answer, you'll give decision-makers ample reason to cut the interview short and you can kiss your promotion goodbye.

2. What Do You Want to Do More Of? Who Needs What You Want to Do More Of?

This is your opportunity to create your ideal promotion or job. Earlier, I described how I did that. If you don't remember the details, please go back to *"My Story"* and refresh your memory before going on to the next question.

3. How Have You Helped Your Employer Achieve Desired Results?

What matters are the results you achieve, not the activities you engage in. Generic 90%ers© take themselves out of contention when they waste decision-makers' time yammering on about their job duties and responsibilities, instead of "tastefully boasting" about what they have accomplished for their companies.

4. How Can You Be the Top Candidate for Promotions for the Rest of your Career?

Here are three things you can do:

1. Get into the habit of keeping your Accomplishments and Skills Data Banks full and current;
2. Only apply where you can be the TOP CANDIDATE. If you can't be the TOP CANDIDATE, what's the point? Save your energy and spirit. Move on.
3. At all times -- Win your Inner Game by keeping your *Lifetime Career Plan©* current (more about this later.)

Your Self-Talk

If your head chatter is an endless negative loop that's killing your Inner Game, you need to work on your Self Talk, the little voice inside you that continually reinforces how great you are, or tells you you're a Victim, or a loser, or worse.

As an HR director and then VPHR, the only people I had ever laid off were documented, poor performers. They were Losers (in my perception for many years.) I also believed Company reorganizations were perfect opportunities to clean out the deadwood.

Then I got laid off.

Immediately, my long-held beliefs and Self-Talk convinced me I too must have been a poor performer, a loser. And six months in outplacement (s-i-x months of being ignored by decision-makers for work I'd proven I could do) reinforced that belief.

I never thought to reframe, or even question, that self-perception; I just kept on believing and reinforcing it. It became a self-fulfilling prophecy that made me an unattractive person. I was always angry, and my Self-Talk made me a potential liability to possible employers.

However, as those 20 CEO invitations began to come in, and later when I got back to work, I was sharply aware of how my Self-Talk changed from Foul to Fabulous, from Loser to Winner, from Victim to Response-Able.

I realized I was 100% responsible for how I felt during all those months after the layoff, as well as for the angry, negative *"I suck!"* vibe I was putting out and that potential employers picked up on, and (rightly) made them avoid me.

Is what I describe also true of you?

For more on this, Google "The Self-Talk Solution" by Shad Helmstetter. You'll find excellent free resources.

Use Your Accomplishments to Win Your "Inner Game"

The quickest and most effective way I know to win your Inner Game and change your self-perception and Self-Talk from whatever it is now to *"I'm a TOP CANDIDATE!!"* is to get very clear and precise on what you have accomplished -- your meaningful, relevant professional and personal accomplishments of which you are most proud or that brought you joy.

These are the ones that brought you joy and moved your Inner Game, your career, and your reputation furthest along.

Separating Generic 90%ers© From Motivated 10%ers©

If you're a Motivated 10%er©, NOW is when you'll begin to distance yourself from the Generic 90%ers© and set yourself up win interviews for the promotions you know you've earned.

Why? Because Generic 90%ers© often mistakenly think their generic résumés convey that they are competent. Big mistake. And unfortunately, they are often too lazy to do what you are about to do: identify in precise terms what relevant accomplishments you have achieved, then prepare yourself to effectively write and authentically speak about them.

When you're done with this course, you'll have Data Banks full of Accomplishment Statements and Skills you can selectively customize to the specific requirements of each promotion you seek.

Get ready. You'll meet a transformed *"New You"* at the end of this course.

For the sake of your success, as you complete BE THE MEATBALL©, please stay focused and stop using your old *job search junk mail©* résumés to apply for opportunities. And remember -- the only promotions you will apply for are those where your accomplishments and skills will make you the MEATBALL, the TOP CANDIDATE.

Assignment #1: Accomplishments of Which You Are Most Proud or that Brought You Joy

Get a little pocket notebook and commit to carrying it with you for the next seven days.

- Think about - AND WRITE DOWN - the personal and professional accomplishments of which you are most proud or that brought you joy.
- Four or five words is all you need for each accomplishment - just enough to jog your memory when you start to write your Accomplishment Essays.
- Ten is a good first target to aim for. Twenty is better. The more, the merrier.

This should be a fun exercise, but sometimes people struggle with it. If you think you might be one of them, don't quit on yourself. It just means this is a new experience for you and you only need to give yourself permission to identify and acknowledge your accomplishments.

Persist. Seven days should do it, but longer if necessary.

My Most Moving Accomplishment Success Story

If you'll let it, this will be an emotionally uplifting and powerful process. Let me give you an example.

When we lived in Seattle, President Obama had just taken office. He inherited a country in a mess — horrible economy and killer unemployment. When he called upon us to share our gifts and help each other out of the mess we were in, I was moved.

I offered a series of free 90-minute résumé workshops to teach people how to create custom résumés to win interviews. In one workshop, when we got to the part where I asked participants to identify the top five accomplishments of which they were most proud, one mid-60s woman from the back row tentatively raised her hand and in a tiny voice said, *"I'm just a waitress. I have no accomplishments."*

"I'm just a waitress. I have no accomplishments."

For a moment, please think about the state of her Inner Game. Maybe even try and feel how she felt about herself. I asked her to please share her story.

She said she had been a waitress at a local truck stop for the past 28 years. The previous week, the owner told everyone not to come to work the next day because he was closing the restaurant at the end of their shift that day.

We all knew the restaurant and we also knew an alliance of local tribes was about to open a 5-star hotel and restaurant in their nearby casino. They were hiring wait staff and she wanted to apply.

Put yourself in her shoes — widow, mid-60s, tipped employee living week-to-week, long-outdated high school education, never had a résumé, suddenly out of work — but with the courage and ambition to go from a greasy spoon truck stop to a 5-star restaurant.

I asked her, if, during those 28 years, parties had come in, placed their orders, and all was good until something went wrong. They were mad and she was expected to fix the problem, and keep them as future customers?

"All the time — part of the job," she said.

I told her she had 28 years of customer service/problem- solving accomplishments, and that 5-star restaurants valued experience like that. Instantly her Inner Game changed from *"Loser"* to *"Winner!!"*

Put yourself in her shoes again — Can you feel, or imagine, how her Inner Game changed in that instant? How different she suddenly felt?

We talked after class and I suggested she identify the top ten "saves" of which she was most proud and apply what she learned in my course to create her résumé and cover letter. And off she went.

Two weeks later I was again giving my presentation. She showed up with her grandson and asked if he could sit in. When we got to identifying everyone's accomplishments, a different woman shot her hand in the air and said in a firm voice, *"I've got something to say."* Taking control of the room, she confidentially repeated her story.

She said she created her custom résumé and cover letter per my instructions, sent them in and was immediately called for an interview, where she learned there were over 500 applicants for just a handful of server jobs. All, she said, were much younger than she was.

A couple of days later the casino called her back for a follow-up interview and hired her. She said she was given full benefits, including retirement, (something she had never had before,) and her tips were two to three times better than her best day during 28 years at the truck stop. And she was thrilled to have her grandson there to witness her pride, share in her happiness and enjoy her tasteful boasting.

She told the class that if they wanted to get back to work, they needed to follow my system.

She had taken a risk on a new system, won her Inner Game, and turned her life around.

Your List of Accomplishments of Which You Are Most Proud or that Brought You Joy

Now it's your turn to do something that I bet most people you know have never done. In case you're struggling, let me share some of the 43 items on my list. Some are recent. Some go back decades, and some are from my childhood. All show a history of relevant facets of me that decision-makers would value, facets that would help make me a TOP CANDIDATE for any opportunity I sought.

Each of these short statements is enough to jog my memory to be able to write a meaningful Accomplishment Essay:

1. Most exemplify Klemmer Samurai Camp values
2. Klemmer SamCamp. My son told class what I meant to him
3. Boy Patrol in 4th grade
4. Earned trust of Aussie banana merchants
5. Succession planning to Australia

6. Identify/plug ongoing annual $2M leak in Australia
7. Basis for ISO 9000 certification in OZ and NZ
8. Direct USAR commission from SP4 to 2LT
9. Researched/wrote original Army area study of Paraguay
10. $13K Top Fundraiser 2005 Charlotte AvonWalk
11. Cigna outplacement of 90 people — all hired
12. Simultaneous interpreter USAR and Marriott
13. While an Army Private, Spanish tutored officers during AIT
14. Wrote PLAN WHILE YOU STILL CAN
15. Took flying lessons in college; soloed three times
16. Diamondback Service key recipient — University of Maryland.
17. As a Freshman, selected to cover Dr. Martin Luther King, Jr. at Howard U.
18. Donated > 24 gallons to Red Cross and counting

I keep my full list handy. Now and again when I feel blah, it's energizing to review the list and rebuild my Inner Game.

I hope you enjoy this time as you learn to *"tastefully boast."* When you're done, put your list aside for a day or so.

Assignment #2: Second Pass - Your List of Accomplishments

Please get your pocket notebook from Assignment 1. It's time to get very focused, give a lot of thought, and finalize your list of the accomplishments of which you are most proud or that brought you joy, because shortly you'll begin creating the blueprint for your future — your Lifetime Career Plan©.

As you review your list, let your mind and spirit drift back. Add new ones that come to mind. Recall the personal and professional accomplishments that filled you with pride, that made your heart sing with joy while you were achieving them. You may have been exhausted when you were done, but it didn't matter because you were alive with the excitement of achievement and tingling with happiness and pride.

You were unstoppable because you and your Inner Game were totally in sync.

I want you to be able to call up —to recreate on demand — those feelings whenever your career hits a wall and you need to restore your Inner Game. Those feelings will be the basis of your Lifetime Career Plan©, and everything begins with the accomplishments of which you are most proud or that brought you joy.

Here are your instructions:

You know the promotion you're seeking – either with your current employer or elsewhere. Which of your accomplishments will make you a perfect TOP CANDIDATE for that specific opportunity?

1. Aim for a list of no less than 20 accomplishments, some personal but mostly professional.
2. Don't forget I asked you to study the final accomplishment statements from selected résumés on my website. Each started as a significant *personal* accomplishment that became a memorable *business* accomplishment. It's time to identify the one you will use for your final one.
3. Don't try to finish the list in one sitting. Commit to keeping the pocket notebook with you for several days. Your subconscious will kick in and start reminding you of past accomplishments. Don't edit. As they come to mind, quickly jot down four or five words to help you remember them later on. And under no circumstances believe you will remember them later. You won't, and you'll miss valuable data.
4. **Reminder:** All you are creating now is the list. You are not yet writing your Accomplishment Essays or Accomplishment Statements.

The Story of Eric and His 10 Friends

We're getting pretty deep into Inner Game, Generic 90%ers©, and Motivated 10%ers©, so by now, you should be aware of an optimistic shift in how you feel about yourself.

To prepare you for what you're about to achieve, let me tell you about my friend Eric and his 10 friends. When Eric and I first met, he was 19 and had just written and published his first book, Action Mentality, available on Amazon. Underemployed (selling children's clothing,) smart, and a super-fast learner, he immediately mastered my system and was able to easily win interviews for better jobs than the one he had when we first met.

We were on the phone late one night and I was sharing my frustration that so many qualified people were mistakenly saying, *"There's no work. Nobody's hiring,"* when there was work and people were being hired - just not them.

They were being ignored for jobs and passed over for promotion interviews because they insisted on using boring generic résumés that gave decision-makers no reason to interview them and made it easy to ignore them.

Eric told me he had shared my first book - *Résumés that Resume Careers* - (See Eric's unsolicited YouTube testimonial – *"Eric Castaneda Testimonial for Résumés That Resume Careers" on YouTube)* with ten of his friends — all "bright pennies" like himself. All were either unemployed or underemployed. He told them to read the book because he was going to mentor all ten of them since he had my system down pat.

All ten read my book. Eight immediately said the process was too hard and went back to their old résumés, the ones decision-makers ignored.

Please take a moment and reflect on the condition of their Inner Games ... Before they even got started, those eight quit on themselves.

The ninth identified a position he was qualified for, followed the system, created a custom résumé and targeted cover letter, and froze.

He refused to submit it because it made him feel "too different." He had done everything necessary to make himself a TOP CANDIDATE, but quit on himself, just when he was poised to take his life to a new level.

Imagine everything those nine could have gained, but instead forfeited because of their losing Inner Games.

The tenth found a position for which his accomplishments and skills made him a TOP CANDIDATE and created a custom résumé and targeted cover letter. He liked how he looked on paper, and more importantly, how he felt about the new person he had become. He applied for the position, and Eric told me that within a week, his tenth friend was interviewed, hired, and started on his new job, and his new life.

Eric's advice to me: *"Don, job seekers are lazy and all they want to do is complain. Forget about the generic 90% and focus on the motivated 10%. Hope that some of the 90%ers see what's happening and cross over but focus on the Motivated 10%."*

Your Lifetime Career Plan©

By now, I hope you're pretty far along in your transformation to Motivated 10%er© and are excited about the future potential benefits for you and your family.

Before we proceed to the last exercise in the first half of the course, please take a few minutes to write down your thoughts on how you see yourself now vs. at the start of the course.

1. Emotional and/or attitudinal transformations?
2. Big Ah-Ha's, maybe around being a Victim?
3. Changes in attitude you have made and are committed to making?
4. Thoughts about the Boilerplate Herd, Generic 90%ers© and Motivated 10%ers©?
5. Your Inner Game now vs. when you started the course?
6. Your job search self-confidence?
7. Anything else?

Please keep those notes handy. They may be handy in the exercise and we'll revisit those questions at the end of the course.

Now, let's complete your transformation by creating your Motivated 10%er **custom Lifetime Career Plan©.** Think of it as your Inner Game Blueprint.

Assignment #3: Create your Custom Lifetime Career Plan©

This final assignment in Part 1 will help you solidify the unstoppable, sustainable feeling of *Winning Your Inner Game.*

If you apply yourself and put your spirit into it, you can *make this blueprint your touchstone* to return to whenever your career hits one of those inevitable roadblocks and you need to reenergize yourself, regain your focus, your job search self-confidence, and win your Inner Game.

Once developed and you've begun your focused search for meaningful work you want to do, your PLAN will help you stay focused and avoid going down unproductive rabbit holes or false start knee-jerk reactions.

Much of what follows comes from Chapter 8 - *How to Win Your Inner Game! Update Your Attitude Before You Update your Résumé.* (Donald M. Burrows, 2014)

Critical Transformative Exercise: Your Lifetime Career Plan©

Everything you've done to this point is to make it possible for you to *believe* you are the TOP CANDIDATE, and act from that belief.

You'll update your PLAN more than once as your career progresses and you mature. No matter what updates you make to your PLAN, what you're about to create will remain the foundation that will help you maintain your Top Candidate mindset for the rest of your career.

Imagine what it would mean to you to be able to recreate an unstoppable feeling, and act from that powerful mindset, for the rest of your career.

Please - Take your time and be thorough as you complete this exercise.

The Lifetime Career Plan© Process

This self-learning exercise is most powerfully and effectively done on a flipchart where you can really see your words appear as you write them; you can also use a notebook or your computer. Here are the four steps:

1. Ideal
2. Actual
3. Obstacles
4. Plan

Divided in half vertically on a flip chart, the left side of the first few pages would be headed

IDEAL	**ACTUAL**	Page #__
A	A	
B	B	
Etc.		

After you have defined the IDEAL and the ACTUAL in as much detail as possible, you'll complete the remaining two categories — OBSTACLES and PLAN.

The final few pages would look like this:

OBSTACLES	**PLAN**	Page #__
A	A	
B	B	
Etc.		

I'll give you an example of a completed PLAN in a moment, but first, here are some guidelines to keep in mind:

1. First, you'll provide as many short answers as possible to this question: *IDEALLY, how do you want to feel as you conduct your search for meaningful work you want to do?*
A.
B.
Etc.

2. Then you'll complete a parallel analysis of each point to answer this question: *ACTUALLY, how you are feeling at the moment?*
A.
B.
C.

You'll complete each category in sequence: IDEAL, then ACTUAL, then OBSTACLES, then PLAN. I encourage you to respond in as much detail as possible. Please record your answers as alphabetical bullet points. When you run out of things to say for the IDEAL, you'll complete a parallel analysis to identify how things are vs. the IDEAL.

In response to the first question *(IDEALLY, how to you want to feel as you conduct your search for meaningful work you want to do?),* don't be satisfied with a lame, generic, superficial answer, like *"I want to feel good"* or *"I want to be happy."* Those answers have no power to move you. They are meaningless air words, just like, *"Have a nice day."*

If you find yourself falling into the air words trap of unthinking generic answers, like *"I want to feel good,"* ask yourself this question: *"What does that mean?"* For each answer, dig more deeply by asking, *"What does that mean?"* until you have no other answer.

For example, you'd ask:

> *"Ideally, how do you want to feel as you conduct your search for meaningful work you want to do? "*
>
> *"I want to feel happy."*

That "air word" answer will not help you:

> *"What does 'feel happy' mean?"*
>
> "Each morning when I wake up, I want to be enthusiastic and optimistic that today is the day they'll want to interview me for the promotion."
>
> *"What does that mean?"*
>
> "I'm excited for them to realize my new résumé proves I'm 100% perfect for the promotion, so they won't ignore me again. For sure they'll interview me this time."
>
> *"What does that mean?"*
>
> "Since I know I'm a TOP CANDIDATE, and I know they only want to interview top candidates, I want to make sure my attitude is 'up' and expectant throughout the day, and my optimism and sincere enthusiasm comes through with each person I meet and each time I answer the phone."

Completing first the IDEAL column and then the ACTUAL, here is how the IDEAL and ACTUAL pages of the flipchart might look.

Please read all of the IDEAL column on the following pages, and then the parallel analysis under ACTUAL.

Step 1. IDEAL	**STEP 2. ACTUAL**
IDEALLY, how do you want to feel as you conduct your search for meaningful work you want to do?	*ACTUALLY, how are you feeling at the moment?*
A. Self-confident and with my self-esteem intact	A. When they talk on the TV news about the economy and a potential recession, I change channels. I psych myself out enough with the "gloom-and-doom" I create for myself – I don't need to hear it from them
B. Believing it will not take long for me to find meaningful work I want to do (in three months, before my savings are gone)	B. My optimism comes and goes. Sometimes I think my situation is just a speedbump and other times I'm terrified I'll never get another good job
C. Upbeat spirit, even in the face of rejection or not ever hearing back from the résumés I submit	C. Nothing works like it used to. Before I could send my résumé to 10 companies and be sure of at least one interview. Now I have sent it to 68 companies, but not one call for an interview
D. "Self-Talk" supportive and empowering	D. My "Self-Talk" sucks. I wish my yappy little voice had laryngitis. The tape that most often plays in my head tells me, "You'll never get another job.

	You're going to be on welfare and food stamps and live under a bridge for the rest of your life."
E. Supported by family and friends and grateful for their referrals and invitations to dinner now-and-again	E. At first, everyone was supportive, optimistic and encouraging. Friends and family would call to check in or invite me over. Now, I feel I make them uncomfortable; they stay away and sometimes look at me funny, like they are embarrassed, or I have a rash on my nose.
F. I can put on a strong, confident, not-desperate "phone face" when I make calls to recruiters and hiring managers	F. I have to psych myself up for every call I make, and the more times I get put down, the harder that is to do. Mostly they ignore me.
G. With enough courage to try non-traditional job search methods, like . . .	G. When I tell people I'm thinking of being a little ballsy and sending my accomplishments résumé and cover letter to CEOs and screw HR (they never respond anyway), people tell me I'm making a mistake. I think it's a cool idea, (nothing else is working) and I'm scared of making a mistake. So, I dither and do nothing.

H. Writing to the CEO to ask for referrals and by-passing HR completely	H. I'm fearful. I keep "updating my résumé" and force it to stay at two pages, but it is just a rehash of the same old "dates-and-duties" crap, and I get no calls for interviews. I can do the job. Companies don't give a damn and yet they complain there's no employee loyalty. No way I can go independent now, but I'd like to. I see the same ad over and over. I applied three times, but they never call
I. Confident I'm not making a HUGE mistake by ignoring people who tell me my résumé "must" be no more than two pages, or that it "must" be in reverse-chronological order	I. Some people say I should include accomplishments in my résumé, but others say HR and recruiters distrust résumés based on accomplishments. I have gaps and a bunch of recent short-term jobs. When I lead with that, I think that's why no one calls. I look like a job jumper. I'm not! It's the

J. Confident in "tastefully boasting" about my accomplishments and skills. My words sound genuine, believable, credible and authentic	J. The local State Job Source office is useless. They insist I use a reverse-chronological résumé, and all the HR departments ignore the résumés thev tell me to
K. Calm, confident, patient and thoughtful in how I run my search, not all panicky and herky-jerky, changing my résumé and approach each time someone hocks up a new opinion	K. My neighbor told me to include an Objective in my résumé; my sister told me her hairdresser told her she read an article in the local paper that an Objective is no longer needed and by omitting it HR would consider me for different jobs. I keep doing what everyone says and still no interviews.
L. Confident my skills and accomplishments are still relevant enough that someone will pay me for what I can do.	L. The longer I'm out, the more obsolete, useless and unemployable I feel. Driving to work, I used to look with curiosity at folks sleeping under the freeway and wonder what it's like to live like that. This keeps up, I'll find out.

So. The first half of the IDEAL PROFILE process is done. What do you think of the information contained in the IDEAL and ACTUAL columns? Does it sound like you?

STRAIGHT TALK. I realize some of the entries are kind of "crunchy" and perhaps you have difficulty imagining yourself writing some of those things. Get over yourself. Now. Just get over yourself and whatever may be left of the "rational lies" you tell yourself.

If you're going to move from being a lost-in-the-crowd-spaghetti-Generic-90%er©, and become a Motivated 10%er© MEATBALL, your first step is to be honest with yourself. Unless you choose to share your PLAN, no one will ever read it. Only you. So please be in integrity with yourself.

After you've finished /IDEAL/ACTUAL/ please give yourself a short break, and then complete /OBSTACLES/PLAN/. To streamline the final two steps, you'll see I've combined multiple /IDEAL/ACTUAL/ items to complete the /OBSTACLES/ column. You don't need to do it that way, but since there were similarities, I chose to combine them. That will carry over into /PLAN/ as well.

STEP 3. OBSTACLES	STEP 4. PLAN
Items A, B, C and D: • I spend too much time in my head, listening to "gloom-and-doom" "Self-Talk" and rehashing my miserable situation • I am rapidly driving myself nuts because I continually focus on all the horrible things that could happen, rather than focusing on solutions.	**A, B, C and D** 1. Explore YouTube for free motivational videos. Spend the first hour of each day playing them and committing to daily affirmations 2. Read Napoleon Hill's *Think and Grow Rich*, and *Law of Success.* Also, watch these links: • Think and Grow Rich • Law of Success 3. For Self-Talk, start with this Shad Helmstetter audio
Items E and F: • My *Self-Talk* again. My self-confidence and self-esteem are the pits. I'm embarrassed about my situations and believe I make others uncomfortable, so they avoid me. And since I feel desperate, I think I	**E and F:** 1. Find the most business-savvy, compassionate, trustworthy and honest person I know. 2. Ask if that person would be willing to review this document and give me their honest feedback?

come across that way to the few recruiters I have spoken to. Nobody wants to interview *"desperate."*	3. If they are willing, ask if they would also role-play some practice interviews with me, give me feedback, and practice again? 4. Stop looking/sending out résumés or requesting *informational interviews.* 5. Stop sending *Job Search Junk Mail©*, finish this process to become Top Candidate.
Items G, H, I and J: • Timid about taking a risk; pay too much attention to what "they" say • When my inner voice says something courageous, I slap it down out of fear and lack of self-esteem • Back away and take shelter again and again inside the *Boilerplate Herd* • I'm uncomfortable being the MEATBALL©; my comfort zone is the **spaghetti.**	**Items G, H, I and J:** 1. Check BizJournals.com and see if they publish a Business Journal for where I want to work. 2. Identify companies of interest to me and create a CEO mailing list. 3. Put together a custom résumé made up ONLY of my most relevant accomplishments and skills, and a targeted cover letter asking for referrals, not a job. 4. Send both to a bunch of CEOs. 5. Really - what harm can it do? Nothing else is working 6. Consider using *The Directory of Executive and Professional Recruiters.*
Item K: Talking myself into an early grave by thinking and doing ineffective things.	**Item K:** 1. Implement this PLAN - not tomorrow. TODAY. NOW!

There! You now have an example of a completed custom Lifetime Career Plan©.

SO THAT YOU CAN SEE HOW ALL 4 COLUMNS CONNECT, I recommend you print out your pages and do a "cut-and-tape."

I wanted to model honest emotion in this real example. So rather than just making stuff up, I drew upon experiences clients have shared with me, and a lot of what I went through when I was laid off and ignored for six evermore fearful months.

After my third interview epiphany, I created and implemented the custom résumé system you are learning, and suddenly had all the interviews I could handle. No reason you won't too. Please be as honest as possible when you complete your /IDEAL/ column. Use my initial /IDEAL/ question or one of your own. If you get the initial question right and are honest with answers, everything flows naturally and effectively.

I know I'm repeating myself, but *please be honest with yourself.* If you are, you'll find the /ACTUAL/ column will be the most difficult because you'll be looking into the mirror of *the current "you"* and you probably won't like what you see. If you're not going to be honest with yourself, what's the point?

If you've been thorough with /ACTUAL/, you'll find the /OBSTACLES/ column may be a little less challenging. Once you've completed it equally thoroughly and honestly, that oppressive weight that you've been carrying around for so long will begin to lift and your spirit will lighten. The /PLAN/ will almost be fun because it's like opening a door from a dark cell and stepping out into light.

I say *"almost"* because you're making a promise to yourself, a commitment, and for this to work for you, you must keep your commitments.

Give a lot of thought to what you're willing to do because I don't want you to quit on yourself. It will please me immensely if you would tell me you saw it through to completion and were successful.

These four columns can be the blueprint to updating your attitude, winning your Inner Game, and getting your career back on-track.

It's time to complete your custom Lifetime Career Plan©

FIRST, please review all the notes you've taken so far. Doing so will refresh your memory, give you food for thought, and help you realize just so how far you've come. Keep your notes handy so you can use them to complete your Plan.

SECOND, please set aside at least three hours of undisturbed time to start and finish your Lifetime Career Plan© without outside interruption – no phones, no pets, no family. Just you. Maybe make it a special event and go to a quiet place that is important to you.

When I lived in Seattle and wanted to do important writing like this, I went to my favorite campsite. This was my view on the Stillaguamish River in the Cascades, and I was just out of cellphone range.

Photo by Don Burrows

Make it a meaningful and important event.

Like any effective plan, it must be fact- and reality-based.

The /IDEAL/, /ACTUAL/ and /OBSTACLES/ are fact- and reality-based. And the /PLAN/ column meets the S.M.A.R.T. criteria of Specific. Measurable. Actionable. Relevant. Timely.

It is also where you get creative and a little daring.

STRAIGHT TALK. I've provided you with a complete Plan to show you how the process works. Under no circumstances should you take what I've written and simply copy it. That's maybe the 'old Generic 90%er© you' – now l-o-n-g behind you.

Instead, I want you to really work to answer this question:

"IDEALLY, how do you want to feel as you conduct your search for meaningful work (promotion or job) you want to do?"

Be aware if you start to feel like a Victim or Imposter. STOP! Don't-Go-There! Do the work. Stretch and dream as you define all the pieces of your /IDEAL/.

Have the courage to honestly feel and face the pain of your /ACTUAL/.

Identify and acknowledge the truth of your /OBSTACLES/, particularly those that you have created through your actions or inactions.

Use /IDEAL/, /ACTUAL/ and /OBSTACLES/ to think broadly, deeply and honestly. Then think expansively to create your custom /PLAN/.

Make use of the resources I provided, but don't limit yourself just to them. Do additional research to find your own resources that will help you create your own CUSTOM Lifetime Career Plan© to expedite your transformation from where you are to where you want to be.

AND as you continue solidifying your Inner Game, here's an additional resource. If you want to fill your heart with joy for all that is good in the world while refocusing on yourself, the Netflix show *Queer Eye* is a wonderful resource. Facebook and Netflix.

Think of all of this as closing a gap.

Have at it.

Take your time. Do good work and get ready to meet a new, more confident "YOU."

~~~~~

Two, maybe three, hours pass as you complete your Lifetime Career Plan©. When you're done, please take a few minutes and write down what you've learned or realized about yourself, what you are thinking and feeling right now.

A bit more time passes... You did do as I asked - yes?

If not, please do so now. This is a critical step in the process and in your quest for the promotion that has been eluding you.

Facts to Remember:

- Motivated 10%ers© do the work and... Trust the process... and win interviews.
- Generic 90%ers© cut corners and... Look for shortcuts... and continue being ignored.
- You get out what you put in.

My Motto:

- *Judge by results. Often harsh. Always fair.*

So, by this point in your transformation, your job search self-confidence — your Inner Game — should be solid. You should have the self-belief and the emotional foundation to win interviews as the TOP CANDIDATE, whenever you want to.

And for those times in the future when you hit a wall and your Inner Game and job search self-confidence get a little dented, you'll know it's only a momentary blip and not your career's death spiral because you can use your Lifetime Career Plan© to quickly re-center yourself in preparation for moving to the next plateau.
~~~~~

With your solid Inner Game and your new *"I'm unstoppable TOP CANDIDATE mindset,"* you're set for Part 2.

You are ready to create the accomplishments and identify the skills that will make you a TOP CANDIDATE and win you interviews for promotions and meaningful work you want to do, from now until you choose to retire

Note: If you want to delve deeper into your Inner Game, Click here for my book, *How to Win Your Inner Game! Update Your Attitude Before You 'Update Your Résumé.'* It and others are available on Amazon and also on my site – topcandidateresumes.com

INTRODUCTION TO PART 2

Your Custom Résumés and Targeted Cover Letters

Introduction

In the second half of the course, you'll:

- Identify and develop your Relevant Professional Accomplishments and the Special Skills and Abilities you used to achieve them;
- Create and fill Accomplishments and Skills Data Banks;
- Create a custom résumé and targeted cover letter based on the specific requirements for the next promotion (or job) you seek;
- Learn to *"tastefully boast"* as you complete your transformation from Generic 90%er© to Motivated 10%er©;
- Meet a *"New, more job-search-self-confident, You."*

When you've mastered what you're about to learn, you'll have everything you need to win interviews as the TOP CANDIDATE for any promotion you seek.

Three TOP CANDIDATE Truths to Remember

1. If you can't get the interview, your education and experience won't matter.
2. If your résumé doesn't give decision-makers a reason to interview you, they won't.
3. No more generic *Job Search Junk Mail©*. Custom résumés and targeted cover letters only, and only apply for promotions (or jobs) where your accomplishments and skills will assure you of being interviewed.

CHAPTER 2

"What Have You Accomplished to Deserve This Promotion?"

During my 18 years of corporate HR management, that was the make-or-break question I loved to ask promotion hopefuls during interviews. The Motivated 10%er© serious contenders had already thought about that question and had answers that were authentic, solid and informative. The Generic 90%ers© winged it and offered up generic platitudes that took them out of consideration.

"What Have You Accomplished to Deserve This Promotion?"

Think about and write out the words you'd use to answer the question.

Having been responsible for managing in-house recruiting, promotions, staffing, compensation, pay-for-performance, merit increases, organization development, management and hourly performance appraisals, and succession planning, I know from experience that more than 90% of promotion-seekers were unable to clearly and effectively state what they had accomplished that earned them the promotions they sought.

They were Generic 90%ers© whose primary (and most ineffective) reason was, *"I've been in my current job for X months/years; I'm entitled to a promotion."*

If you recognize yourself in that answer, here is the Rude Awakening.

NO! You were not entitled to a promotion. You were entitled to be paid for the work you did. And you were. The scale is balanced.

Time-in-grade counts for pension purposes but does not entitle you to a promotion.

The only time you've earned a promotion is when you have consistently gone over-and-above what's expected, outperformed your competition, and hopefully, made decision-makers aware of it.

That's the reality and the truth. Make it a foundational belief of the rest of your career and strive to live the truth.

As a Motivated 10%er, while winning the promotion is your immediate goal, your longer-term objective should be to stop making yourself invisible and instead make yourself indispensable, so you'll be top-of-mind for high-visibility assignments and promotions, and be the last on the lay-offs list in the next recession.

Motivated 10%ers© think in terms of accomplishments, and therefore are valuable to the company. They survive layoffs, downsizing, rightsizing, restructuring, reorganizations — call it what you will — and they will always get the best assignments.

Generic 90%ers©, those who do just enough to get by but don't know and cannot articulate their value to the company, present themselves in terms of their job duties and activities. When push comes to shove, they have made themselves expendable. Your best chance of bullet-proofing your career is to be a Motivated 10%er©.

Motivated 10%ers© are valuable to their employers. Not only do they survive layoffs, they get the cool special assignments, and they win promotions. And yes, I'm repeating myself. I want to make certain you hear me. This point is critical to your career.

Values Transformation Inventory

The next step in your transformation is to get clear on WHAT you are willing to do, and WHO you're willing to become, to be the TOP CANDIDATE each time you apply - from now until you retire.

To do that, you'll figure out what you bring to the *World of Work*.

Not to your current job, but to the *World of Work*.

Here come the questions. Superficial thinking is not permitted. Think deeply. Take your time.

Please review your Lifetime Career Plan©, make any updates or edits necessary to strengthen it, bring it current, and make it an honest reflection of who and where *you* are right now.

Then -- Please answer these five questions.

1. What are you willing to do to always be the TOP CANDIDATE? For example, you might be willing to:
   A. Learn how, and what, your job truly contributes to your company's profitability
   B. Learn to always define yourself in terms of specific measurable accomplishments, not just your daily activities
   C. Separate yourself from the Boilerplate Herd. Get out of your blend-in, spaghetti comfort zone so you can build your career around STAND-OUT MEATBALL
   D. Create and keep your Accomplishments and Skills Data Banks always up-to-date so you're always ready to quickly take advantage of unexpected opportunities
   E. Intentionally keep yourself focused on accomplishments and develop a TOP CANDIDATE mindset by reviewing your accomplishments weekly. Always be on the alert to identify needs going unmet, and be ready, willing, and able to present yourself as the custom solution to those needs.

Those are just examples - What are YOU willing to do?

2. As you look back over your career since your last promotion, what specific things have you done to deserve your next promotion? Or has your career been on "cruise control"?
3. Over the last two years, how, specifically, have you created maximum value for others?
4. Assuming you have not yet developed into the person you'd ultimately like to become, what new traits and skills do you want to acquire, and what's your plan to do so? How committed are you to your list? Why?

   Again, think deeply. Don't just settle for the first superficial and obvious thoughts that flit into your mind — i.e. *"to make more money."*

5. **Considering all facets of you and your career to this point—If where you are now is your life's FIRST BASE, what does SECOND BASE look like?** (And please understand that when you get to SECOND BASE, it then becomes your new FIRST BASE.)

To make sure I've explained the concept clearly, let me use myself as an example.

Right now, my FIRST BASE is that I am comfortably retired and am creating this course because I want to leave a legacy for my kids, something to mark my time on earth, one that helps stalled mid-career professionals progress in their careers, and ultimately does away with the idea that résumés can only be two-page reverse-chronological format.

My SECOND BASE would be this:

- BE THE MEATBALL© has destroyed the traditional, two-page, generic reverse-chronological *"dates-and-duties"* job search junk mail© template résumé. Generic 90%ers have become Motivated 10%ers and recruiters and decision-makers expect to only interview applicants with TOP CANDIDATE mindsets and custom résumés,
- No one is ignored for work they can do or passed over for promotions they've earned because they have the job search self-confidence to BE THE MEATBALL©,
- The careers of people who apply this course take off like rockets,
- BE THE MEATBALL© goes viral as people develop MEATBALL mindsets, self-awareness, self-appreciation, pride, and job search self-confidence,
- People like the waitress who define themselves *as "I'm just a... ,"* no longer do.

When that SECOND BASE becomes my new FIRST BASE, then my new SECOND BASE would be to translate my course into Spanish, conduct webinars in Spanish from my home, and from time-to-time run live workshops in México.

Assignment #4: Five Questions

Answer all five of the preceding questions. Please don't rush. Move ahead only when you've completed the exercise to your Motivated 10%er© level of excellence.

This is your chance to design your future by answering just five questions.

Two Concurrent Assignments to Get Started on Now: Part B & Text Column, Left Side, Page 1

Part B

Part B is a copy-and-paste Word doc containing your work history, education, military service (if applicable), certificates, licenses, publications, and such. It anticipates and answers questions about gaps in your employment history, and once you get it the way you like it, it will not change from résumé to résumé.

Sequentially, Part B appears after the Representative Professional Accomplishments section and completes your custom résumé. You saw examples under *Successes* in topcandidateresumes.com. Please take a few minutes and review those 12 résumés now, before you go any further.

Give thought to your Part B because effectively presented, it will help make you unique, not just another blend-in strand of spaghetti.

It generally takes some time to get Part B the way you like it, so please get started on it now. Ideally, you'll have it done when you complete the course.

Please click here and study the different Part Bs (TopCandidateResumes.com/successes).

Points to keep in mind:

1. Particularly in difficult job markets, not only do you want your résumé to stand out, **you want it to anticipate and answer decision-makers' questions, not raise them.** You may be qualified for the promotion you seek, but a sloppy or incomplete

Part B will often cause your résumé to end up in the decision-maker's *Thanks-But-No-Thanks* file.

2. **Everything you put here is verifiable**. Don't fake (read: lie) anything.

3. **Decision-makers and screeners who are paying attention will pay attention to your dates of employment**. Inconsistencies or unexplained gaps here are a primary reason why they'll pass you over in favor of other applicants. Don't make them wonder.

4. **Be sure to account for all time frames**. It's painful to the interviewer and disconcerting for the applicant to have fill in the gaps on-the-spot. The interviewer gets fidgety, wondering what else you have omitted, and think maybe it's time to end the interview and move on to others who have their acts together.

5. **Show both beginning and ending month and year for all jobs, education, military service, and other items with start and end dates.** Just putting the years without the months causes doubt about your integrity - like did you join the company in January or December of 2017 and leave in January or December of 2018? It makes a difference. With so many qualified people looking, you must do all you can to make yourself the TOP CANDIDATE

6. **Education. If you had a good GPA (3.0 or better on 4.0 scale,) I recommend you include it**, even if you graduated a while ago. It shows long-term commitment to achieve a goal

7. **Recognition/Activities.** Dean's List? Put it in. Officeholder in the dorm or campus organizations? Put it in. Service Key for writing on the campus daily? Put it in. Special recognition? Put it in. Paid your way through school by working in the cafeteria? What percent? Put it in. You get the idea.

All of these speak volumes about **positive character traits** that employers will value., but they'll never know about them if you don't put them in. All can be turned into effective talking points and accomplishments of interest to current and potential employers.

If your GPA was less than a 3.0 but you worked a bunch of hours each week to put yourself through school, give yourself credit. That should be in your Accomplishments Data Bank and Part B.

And if your GPA was less-than-impressive because you partied your way through school, don't try to BS your way around it. Turn it into a positive growth experience.

Own up to it, and make sure you can share a "lesson learned" from it — maybe something like, *"Looking back on those years, it was a wonderful time of new-found freedom, personal growth, defining boundaries, and learning what worked, and what didn't. Once I got the 'party hearty' bug out of my system, I buckled down and learned to focus. For example, ... "*

And then make sure you have a meaningful, relevant learning example that relates to the opportunity you are seeking.

Relevant facets of you. Your résumé is intended to show all relevant facets of you until you are face-to-face with decision-makers and can speak for yourself.

Something that you take for granted and without thinking omit from your résumé could be the tipping point for favorable consideration.

When I was in university, I wrote for the school daily and took journalism and photography electives because they were interesting.

When I finished grad school, my father wrote my first résumé and included writing and photography in it. I challenged that because I thought personal interests had no place in a business document. What did I know?

The Marriott Hotels recruiter had circled "Photography" in red, about 135 times.

Turned out that in my first job out of school (property personnel director at the Miami Marriott), Corporate Communications liked it when personnel directors wrote articles and took photos of employee events for in-house publications. Article-writing and photography weren't job requirements but having the abilities to do both was a strong plus. Maybe even the tipping point in my favor because I had zero hotel or Human Resources knowledge or experience.

QUESTION: What are all the *relevant facets of you* that could be your tipping points?

Please get started on your Part B so it is done when you finish your résumé.

Text Column - Page 1 / Left

Your other parallel assignment is your *Text Column – Page 1 / Left.*

You'll find several examples of dramatic Text Column content on résumés under SUCCESSES on my website. Use them for inspiration as you decide on the **highlights of you** that you want to showcase.

It's OK if there's selective repetition of critical information in the Text Column and elsewhere in your résumé.

Please dedicate focused thought and time to decide what you want to include in the Text Column. That critical space should make a visually dramatic TOP CANDIDATE first impression.

Here's an effective Text Column. Click here to check out E.C.'s Text Column and the rest of her résumé.

Her Text Column is an eye-catching summary of the unique things she brought to her next promotion, things she may not have shared with decision-makers before but may now want to.

Content for your Text Column is free-form.

E.C. told me her Text Column impressed decision-makers and contributed to her winning her promotion to her current position.

Assignment #5: Part B and Text Column

Start creating your both your Part B and your Text Column now, and tinker with them until they present all the relevant facets of you.

CHAPTER 3

Your Representative Professional Accomplishments

You'll accomplish a lot in this chapter. You'll:

1. Learn to differentiate between an *activity* and an *accomplishment*
2. Finalize your list of accomplishments
3. Write accomplishment essays on selected accomplishments
4. Analyze your essays for completeness
5. Write accomplishment statements from your essays
6. Play the "So What? Game"©
7. In addition to your professional accomplishments, you'll identify one personal accomplishment to convert into your final professional accomplishment.

Differentiating Between an Activity and an Accomplishment

To grab a decision-maker's attention and win an interview, your résumé must be packed with accomplishments relevant to the opportunity you seek, not generic activities.

Please, learn from this true story.

The résumé I'm going to refer to is the first one under *Successes* on my website, topcandidateresumes.com.

Greg, a brilliant engineer, had a 48-hour window to apply for a division director of engineering job that was only about 238% perfect for him.

He sought my help to create a résumé and cover letter customized to the requirements of the position and make the deadline.

This was the first accomplishment in the résumé he had created for himself. *"Developed system specifications/requirements from customer want list."*

He thought that was an accomplishment.

It wasn't.

It was a significant activity that resulted in the real accomplishment.

When I read an activity that someone mistakenly calls an accomplishment, my first reaction is to play the "So What?" Game.

I don't mean *"So what?"* in a snarky or combative tone, but rather in a questioning, interested, *"Well, so what else? Tell-me-more"* conversational tone.

What follows is a hypothetical example of a "So What?" conversation to turn that activity into an effective and memorable accomplishment statement. As you read through the example, remember the funnel, or imagine going down a set of stairs.

The top step is an activity. It is wide-open, general, and generic. By the time we get to the bottom step, we're very specific and have arrived at the essence of the accomplishment statement.

Top Step:

> He: "I developed system specifications/requirements from customer want list."
>
> Me: "So what?"

Second Step:

> He: "The customer wanted us to create prototypes of large, next-generation sensors they were developing. They had a wish-list of over 300 specifications and requirements, but the list was not as specific as we needed it to be. Before I could work on the prototype, I needed to understand the big picture and create a usable document of their requirements/specification."
>
> Me: "So What?"

Third Step:

> He: "I spent one full day on-site meeting with the client. I was able to ask all my questions and get very clear on their expectations.

They also gave me a copy of their design drawings. Back in my office, I loaded all of their data into a software program I created and developed the required information. Since my program enables me to cost out parts, I took some more time and as a value-add for the client, created a new parts list too. In all, I spent four days on this assignment.

As I reviewed the design drawings, I noticed three errors that, if Manufacturing followed the design, I knew the prototype would fail. As tactfully as possible, I brought them to the client's attention. They were embarrassed and grateful.

We won the 7-figure contract and I later learned that my contribution to the process was what made them choose our company."

See how that goes?

If you're on the alert for lazy thinking and will make it an unbreakable habit not to settle for the first (and often imprecise, superficial) thought that comes along, and instead commit to playing several rounds of the "So What?" Game©, you'll generate a ton of relevant information.

And from that information, he could write up this engaging accomplishment statement:

"A potential customer came to us to make prototypes of their large state-of-the-art next-generation sensor system for use in civilian aircraft. They had an extensive but disorganized wish list of specifications and requirements they wanted built into the prototype. I was assigned the task of bringing order to their wish list. I spent one day in on-site meetings with engineers and managers to get very clear on their expectations, and another three days completing my analysis and the assignment. Reviewing their engineering drawings, I found three design errors that would cause the prototype to fail. I advised the client and they were grateful. Using a program I had written, I completed the project, and as a value-added service, included parts cost data as well. We won the 7-figure contract. I was later told that my contribution was the deciding factor in choosing us."

That's an effective 143-word accomplishment statement, to store in his Accomplishment Statements Data Bank, ready for customization as needed to become the Top Candidate for future opportunities.

If you're pressed for time, playing "So What?" is a viable short-cut to quickly turn an activity into an accomplishment.

And, if you're wondering, he won the division director of engineering job. I should also tell you he was the youngest of the five finalists. And finally, I should tell you his résumé was four pages long.

Right. *Four pages.*

Now if you're still got a little doubting Boilerplate Herd, Generic 90%er© going, you're probably saying or thinking something like, *"Four pages! Nobody will read four pages!"*

And really, you'd be about 100% wrong.

The CEO, who never interviewed candidates at this level but just looked at résumés of the finalists, devoured every word of his custom résumé, and targeted cover letter, then *demanded* to meet the engineer who thought in such a "disruptive" manner. And then he hired him.

The other four finalists on the final list were all Generic 90%ers©, and as you know by now, Generic 90%ers© are a dime-a-dozen. The CEO ignored all of them.

Poof!

When you read these Success Stories, count the pages in each résumé.

If you still have some old Generic 90%er© bias hanging around, please accept my invitation to get out of your own way and join other Motivated 10%ers©.

Your List of Accomplishments

To fill your Accomplishments Data Bank quickly, please DO NOT have a specific promotion in mind as you develop your list of accomplishments and then write your essays.

Right now, all you are doing is completing an inventory, making a list of the accomplishments of which you are most proud or that brought you joy, the ones you loved doing, moved your career furthest along, and want to do more of. Later you'll identify the corresponding skills that you used to achieve them, the skills you bring to the World of Work.

JUST TO BE CLEAR: It's not yet time to create a custom résumé, nor are you seeking a specific promotion or job.

Instead, you're about to have a lot of fun getting clear on your relevant professional accomplishments, meeting a "New You" and becoming comfortable with your reasons for *"tastefully boasting."*

As you finish your list, give a lot of thought to ***your most memorable personal accomplishment***, the one you'll convert into an even more memorable professional accomplishment.

As a Motivated 10%er©, you'll enthusiastically aim for a minimum of 20 accomplishments.

Activity: Finish Your List of Accomplishments

Please finalize your list before going any further.

An Example of an Accomplishment Essay

OK. Your final list of accomplishments is done.

To explain the remaining steps, I'm going to dip into material from three of my books:

1. How to Win Interviews! Stop Sending Job Search Junk Mail
2. Burn Your Résumé – You Need a Professional Profile, co-authored with Deborah Drake, and
3. "O" is for Objective - 4 Steps to Be the Ideal Candidate. All are available on Amazon and on my site.

Here's an example of an effective accomplishment essay by my friend Gerald Grinter, author of The Art of Working for Yourself. The word count is 278, close enough to 250 for me.

As you read the essay, visualize a funnel and notice how the content goes from very wide to very narrow — like a funnel. Keeping the funnel in mind should help you focus your writing.

> "I had a friend of mine refer his plumber to me as a possible client. From the first time we met, he said he wasn't trying to do anything fancy for his business. He was a no-frills type of guy. As a matter of fact, he even refused to talk to me because he wasn't sure he needed anything.
>
> He had been a plumber for over 25 years and knew his trade inside and out. Then the company he worked for let him go after working for them for over 15 years. He called me wanting to know what he should do to start his own plumbing business.
>
> After getting his business license and corporate entity in place, we set out to create a web page for him and develop a basic social media strategy. This was no small feat for a plumber. Usually, when someone says they want a website they bring you all sorts of pages and ideas but working with contractors and plumbers is a different language and style all its own. Luckily, I had a little experience with contractors from my days in commercial insurance. So, I used that knowledge to create a starting point for his website and social media plan.
>
> We put together a Facebook fan page and added his business listing to Yelp. Not long after he called and was pretty excited to let me know he got his first Yelp referral after being listed for a few weeks.
>
> This was music to my ears. He was on his way. Now he is so busy we can hardly meet to update his pages. But I guess that is a good thing."

Writing a well-thought-out essay will help you think through your accomplishments and prepare you to interview more effectively.

Your Accomplishments Essays

Now we're getting into the essence of the second half of the book.

Now that your list is done, it's time to:

- Decide which accomplishments are the ones you loved achieving and want to do more of in your new promotion or new job. Aim for between 8 and 10.
- **For each of those 8 – 10 accomplishments**, write a tightly-focused accomplishments essay of about 250 words. You'll answer these four questions: *WHAT I did? HOW I did it? WHY I did it?* and *What were the QUANTIFIED RESULTS of what I did?*

Your other accomplishments, those that don't match the requirements for this opportunity you seek, will remain in your Accomplishments Data Bank for future opportunities. At some point, you'll likely have reason to write the full essays, just not right now.

Activity: Write Your Essays Now

Time now to write all of the essays you will use for the promotion or position you seek.

Remember: Your target is ~ 250 words per essay

Stop reading. Start writing.

~~~~~ Time Passes

Analyze Accomplishment Essays for Completeness

If you use Microsoft Word, you can easily analyze your essay by using the Review/New Comment tool and the Comment bubbles that will appear in the right margin. If you don't know what I'm talking about, now would be a good time to get acquainted with your tool.

Ideally, each of your essays will answer all four of the questions. That doesn't always happen, so when you use this process, you can catch omissions. I have extracted sentences from Gerald's essay and separated them with these marks: //

Here are the sentences I believe best answer the four questions:
~~~~~

WHAT I DID? //"After getting his business license and corporate entity in place we set out to create a web page for him and develop a basic social media strategy // create a starting point for his website and social media plan. We put together a Facebook fan page and added his business listing to Yelp"//

WHY I DID IT? //"Then the company he worked for let him go after working for them for over 15 years. He called me wanting to know what he should do to start his own plumbing business."//

HOW I DID IT? //"Luckily I had a little experience with contractors from my days in commercial insurance. So, I used that knowledge to create a starting point for his website and social media plan."//

QUANTIFIED RESULTS OF WHAT I DID? //"Not long after he called and was pretty excited to let me know he got his first Yelp referral after being listed for a few weeks. // Now he is so busy we can hardly meet to update his pages."//

After Analyzing your essays for completeness, please keep the essays and analyses in a Word doc called ACCOMPLISHMENT ESSAYS.

Activity: Analyze Your Essays for Completeness

Analyze all of your essays now.

Edit as needed to answer all four questions.

Your Accomplishment Statements

Your *Accomplishment Statements* are tightly-worded statements summarizing the Accomplishment Essays.

As you identify different opportunities for using a specific Accomplishment Essay, please don't be lazy and just use the last Statement you wrote. It worked for the last opportunity you sought.

For it to work again, customize it again.

The **accomplishment statement target is six sentences.** Around 120 - 140 words. Make sure you've answered all four questions (WHAT? HOW? WHY? QUANTIFIED RESULTS?)

Before I start writing an accomplishment statement, I think about the essence of the accomplishment and try to capture that in my first sentence. The tone of the essay should be conversational, not stilted or forced. The words in the first sentence don't have to come from the essay; generally, they don't.

I try to end with RESULTS, but I don't follow any set order in answering the four questions. It's based on the content of each essay and is a question of personal preference and style. After you've written a few, you'll learn what's most effective for you. Don't settle for your first try.

I generally make my opening sentence broad and summarize the essence of the situation. I get more focused as I progress with the rest of the statement.

Like a funnel.

Since you've already written the details in the Accomplishment Essay, don't rehash them here in your Accomplishment Statement. You want the short version. Back to Gerald. Here's his final accomplishment statement.

The same funnel structure still applies. Notice how the first sentence summarizes the situation.

> "Self-employed tradesmen are sometimes hesitant to acknowledge and seek out small business consulting and coaching, even when the need is immediate. Such was the case with a plumber that a friend referred to me. He had 25 years' experience and after 15 years with a company, was laid off and decided he was ready to take responsibility for his career. Having never had a reason to develop business, marketing and social media plans, website, and related items, this was not an easy system for him to embrace. Yet we persevered, and within a few weeks of getting things set up, he got his first referral

> from YELP. Now he is so busy we can hardly meet to update his web page. Another business up and running."

A compact little 126-word story that will engage the reader and remind them of similar problems they too may have. It makes the sender authentic and memorable.

Contrast Gerald's focused statement with a generic statement, like *"I'm a business consultant, and I help people set up websites."*

If you were a plumber just getting started, which of the two statements would attract your attention: the generic business consultant's activities statement, or Gerald's?

Activity: Write All of Your Accomplishment Statements

As with your accomplishment essays, it's time to stop reading and start writing.

Your target for each accomplishment statement is between 120 and 140 words.

Have at it.

Activity: Play The "So What?" Game©

The "So What?" Game© lets you make sure you've answered the four questions in both your Accomplishment Essay and Statement, and what you've written really is an accomplishment and not just a bunch of generic activities.

As a reminder, a résumé filled with activities is nothing more than *Job Search Junk Mail©*, and you know what you do with junk mail at home.

Play "So What?" on each of your accomplishment statements, before proceeding to the next section.

Your One *Personal* Accomplishment to Convert into Your Final Professional Accomplishment

In addition to Part B and your Text Column, there is one other item that will remain unchanged from one résumé to the next: your personal/professional accomplishment statement.

With some imagination, many of your personal accomplishments can be turned into valuable professional assets that make you positively memorable to decision-makers.

And when they like you before they've even met you, you're half-way to hired.

For example: when you checked out this résumé on my site, I hope you read and recall this final accomplishment statement on Jen Haga's résumé:

> COST-CONSCIOUS, HANDS-ON CREATIVITY
>
> After planning everything to the nth degree, I experienced the BEST THREE DAYS OF MY LIFE—my wedding. From the tiara to the train of my dress to the table arrangements — I planned everything and had hands-on involvement in most of it as well. Everything within my control went just as I had envisioned it. Why is my wedding an accomplishment for my résumé? Because by utilizing my contacts within the industry and the area, and by doing many things myself, I created an elegant $15,000 wedding for only $8,371 - a savings of $6,629. *I promise you I am just as detail-oriented and cost-conscious when it comes to spending my employer's money as I am with my own.*

While her résumé was full of relevant professional accomplishment statements that caught the interest of decision-makers, this was the final statement, placed there intentionally so it would be the last, and most memorable, thing people read and remembered about her.

That 121-word personal accomplishment became a memorable professional accomplishment statement.

People looked forward not just to interviewing her, but to getting to know her because her résumé made her interesting. Even before meeting her, decision-makers liked her, and that put her miles ahead of her Generic 90%er© competition.

And in her testimonial on the back cover of this book, she said, *"Had it not been for Don's process I would not have been a candidate for the position I have today. I didn't have the experience that the position required but by providing my boss with my accomplishments she saw that I had the capacity to do the job."*

Note: I realize Jen's testimonial appears to contradict my advice to only apply where you can be the top candidate. As you'll see when we get to cover letters, she was not applying for a specific position, but rather was using my strategy tap into her network and *seek referrals* to places and people where she might fit.

Another Example

Let's say you're a recent MBA graduate seeking your first marketing management job out of grad school. Would you have thought to end your résumé with an accomplishment focusing on an illness?

Generic 90%ers©? No way. They're *"Spaghetti thinkers"* and would be content to just list their dates and job duties and call it good.

BUT a Motivated 10%er© who knows the value of being the "MEATBALL" and has mastered this system, definitely would.

Alejandro is from México, and English is his second language. Here's the last accomplishment statement on his résumé. His cover letter is in Spanish; his résumé is in English.

> **High Sense of Commitment and Perseverance**
> Due to a necessary medical treatment with cortisone for 6 years, I reached a level of morbid obesity. Today I can say that with commitment, persistence, and perseverance I lost 115 pounds 7 years ago and have never rebounded. I promise to have the same commitment and efficient results-oriented mindset with you as I

am achieving my own personal goals. No matter how hard they might seem.

Impressive commitment.

Decision-makers thought so too. The last time we were in contact, Alejandro had been promoted twice and was his company's sales director in Panamá. Using the generic job search junk mail© template résumé and job search strategies pushed by his university placement office, he went six months without an interview.

Those employers who ignored him had no idea what they were missing. He can now get interviews whenever he wants them.

It's all in how you choose to see yourself and present yourself.

Want the Interview? Be the Meatball, not the spaghetti. ©

CHAPTER 4

Your Special Skills and Abilities & Custom Objective Statement

Your next step is to identify your Special Skills and Abilities, and you have a choice: You can either do it immediately upon completing each Accomplishment Essay, or you can complete both the Essay and the Statement, and then analyze both to identify the Special Skills and Abilities you used to achieve each accomplishment.

Your call.

Would You Agree that Your Skills and Abilities Make You Who You Are?

I believe that you are the sum of two kinds of skills: your **transferrable skills** (applicable in many different jobs and circumstances) and your **motivated skills** (the ones you love to use and when you do, you get your best results.)

I also believe that over the years you've earned promotions that require you to **use your motivated skills**. And if you've never taken the time to precisely identify those skills, you are at a disadvantage if you want to take charge of your career.

We'll fix that now.

The goal is for you to accurately know the skills and abilities you used to achieve your accomplishments, and to be able selectively present them concisely, authentically, effectively, and compellingly in your cover letter and résumé, and then be able to support them intelligently in interviews.

As in-house recruiter and hiring manager, I didn't want to hire or promote blah people, mediocre *"maintainers,"* folks who would just take up space, and in the future become organizational deadwood.

I wanted people who could grow and add value to the company. To identify them, it was important for me to understand an applicant's level of self-awareness.

My preferred way to do that was to ask them to tell me about the most significant skills they used to achieve their accomplishments.

If you and I were in a promotional interview and I asked you the very open-ended question, *"Tell me about your most significant skills"*, how would you answer?

Please stop and write out the words you'd use to answer that question.

This is a perfectly fair question, and a critically important one for you to answer effectively.

If, before we interviewed, you had thought deeply and thoroughly about your skills, (what you bring to the *World of Work*) and were prepared to respond convincingly and authentically, the question would have been a gift and you'd have an opportunity to hit a home run.

You'd begin to separate yourself from your competition, moving from just another faceless generic *applicant* floating in the applicant pool to a potentially promising *candidate* up on the candidate slate.

Of course, the flip side is true as well. If you gave a blah generic answer, you'd have just blown a fine opportunity to separate yourself from your competition.

Evidentially, *"Tell me about your most significant skills"* is harder than I thought because the majority of applicants would gaze fixedly at the ceiling and finally respond with something vague, generic, and completely unimpressive, like, *"I'm a people person"* or *"I'm really good in math"* or *"I'm very well-organized."*

True, for sure. But *generic answers* to important *specific questions* are unimpressive.

When applicants get passed over for promotions or ignored for jobs, many careers drown in applicant pools.

Do You Know What You Bring to the "World of Work"?

Deborah Drake, my writing partner in another life, wrote in our book, *Burn Your Résumé. You Need a Professional Profile,* "We imagine you think you know who you are and what your skills are. With complete respect for your opinion, our experience leads us to differ with you. When was the last time you took a complete and honest personal inventory of your accomplishments and the skills you used to achieve them? You may not currently know all of the real "you" if it has been some time, or never."

Are You Living in A Rut?

All too often we impose our own very artificial, imaginary limits on the jobs or projects we think we can, and cannot, do. We often (wrongly) think that since we have always done one particular kind of job or project, that's all we are qualified to do.

When you've finished identifying the Special Skills and Abilities you used to achieve your Representative Professional Accomplishments, you'll see that many of your essential skills are applicable in a variety of work and business situations.

When Was the Last Time You Completed A Detailed Skills Inventory?

A moment ago, I referenced Deborah's observation regarding how well you think you know yourself and the completion of a **skills inventory.**

Identifying your most relevant accomplishments, writing your essays and creating your accomplishment statements was the first half of that **personal inventory**. The **Skills Analysis/Identification process** you are about to complete is the second half.

Can you see what an advantage clearly knowing your skills will give you over your Generic 90%er© competition, who still use activity-based, generic, dates-and-duties spaghetti résumés?

Free Online Resources

There are a number of free skills identification resources available on-line.

I think this one is particularly helpful: https://www.careeronestop.org/Toolkit/Skills/skills-matcher-questions.aspx.

It is sponsored by the US Department of Labor. I encourage you to complete the four-page questionnaire. It will take less than 10 minutes.

I tried it and found it accurate. Based on your responses, it will give you a list of careers and salary ranges that matched your self-assessment.

You'll also receive an unexpected bonus. To the left of the jobs, in the box titled YOUR SKILLS, you'll find a link called *"See Your Full List of Skills"*. There I found a comprehensive, downloadable list of the skills related to my responses to their questions.

Assignment #6: Identify Your Transferrable Skills

After you've completed the exercise, please print out your full list of skills. Edit the list as you see fit.

Then create a table like this:

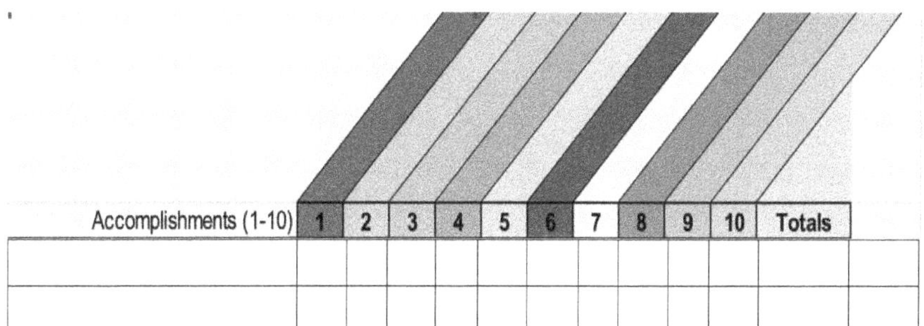

Accomplishments (1-10)	1	2	3	4	5	6	7	8	9	10	Totals	

Vertical column: Your Skills. Diagonals: Your Accomplishment Essays

Working on only one accomplishment essay at a time, go down the list reading each skill in turn. If you used it in the achievement of that accomplishment, put a ✯ in the corresponding box and column. After you have completed the first essay, follow the same process for your remaining essays.

Total the number of stars in each row and enter that number under Totals.

Rank-order the skills in the empty far-right column.

When you have finished analyzing all of your essays, the stars will create a profile of the transferrable skills and abilities you have used to achieve your most significant accomplishments.

I believe you'll be surprised at the number of skills you have stared.

Create a Word document for your **Transferrable Skills Data Bank** that contains all of your transferrable skills. Organize them in whatever way is most effective for you.

Motivated Skills

Assignment # 7 - Identify your Motivated Skills.

From your list of Transferrable Skills, identify a handful – maybe eight to ten – that you love to use, and require your best efforts.

These are your MOTIVATED SKILLS. You want your next opportunity to require you to use as many of them as possible. Please refer back to "My Story" earlier in the book.

Create a separate Word doc for your Motivated Skills. Have you made an honest self-assessment? If you have, I'd like you to please remember the following observation:

Geoffrey Bellman writes in *The Consultant's Calling*, "We should be able to look our strengths as well as our weaknesses in the eye. When others are interested, we should be able to articulate who we are and what we do well, and own up to who we are not and what we do not do well. Thinking about when and how to bring our talents to the workplace should provoke more excitement than anxiety. A confident self-assessment helps on all these levels."

You have now completed that self-assessment. Please create your **Motivated Skills Data Bank**.

Note: *Please understand that this is not a one-shot deal to create a new résumé.*

To be the TOP CANDIDATE for the rest of your career, you must keep adding to your Accomplishment Statements and Skills Data Banks so you will always have a ready supply of material you can **Selectively Customize** to make yourself the TOP CANDIDATE when yet another perfect promotional opportunity appears.

... And as you will recall - if you can't be the TOP CANDIDATE, what's the point? Save your energy. Don't bother applying.

Custom Objective Statement

Three Elements of an Effective Custom Objective Statement

1. Exact title of the promotion sought,
2. Two or three of the essential requirements of the promotion that you absolutely meet,
3. Your unique contribution of the position, showing your awareness of their need going unmet, a need the employer does not know they have, that you can fill.

In a moment, you'll read seven actual custom Objective Statements I copied-and-pasted from client résumés on my site.

Each followed my system, and as you'll see by the different formats, fonts and content, each added their unique spin to what they wrote.

Seven Examples of Custom Objective Statements

New Position and Promotion:

OBJECTIVE: Director of Engineering for COMPANY NAME / DIVISION / PRODUCT, a position requiring significant project management, hardware and software research and development experience, metrics-based people management skills, and a deft touch to mentor and develop staff.

Promotion within the company:

OBJECTIVE

Seeking a project management position within [COMPANY] that will utilize over a decade of proven experience in successful project management, business analytics, and customer service.

Marketing Management position (first job out of college):

Objective: A Marketing Position for X COMPANY in which I am expected to perform analysis of problems and needs, planning projects, creating cost-effective solutions for the company, conceptualizing new ideas to be ahead of the market, service management, design and budget control as well as to establish strategic valuable relationships for the company.

Promotion to first job out of US Navy (Enlisted):

OBJECTIVE: F/A-18 Egress/Environmental Systems Technician Level II. Install, remove, replace. service, adjust and troubleshoot ejection seat, canopy, explosive devices, airframe/avionics related environment control systems, and functional components including rigging of explosive linkage devices, ejection seat, canopy, canopy drive and locking mechanisms using hand tools, power tools and applicable test equipment. Performing hourly, calendar, phase and conditional inspections as required by maintenance requirement cards.

Promotion and return to prior employer:

OBJECTIVE: VICE PRESIDENT, CUSTOMER SUCCESS in a small to medium-sized company requiring expert Project Management skills, a relentless commitment to management by metrics, and an abiding desire to mentor and develop staff

MY MOTTO: I NEVER "DON'T." ***I ALWAYS "DO"***

Promotion for Army officer returning to civilian life:

OBJECTIVE: Project Manager – Texas Children's Hospital, a position requiring extensive experience in leading work teams, ability to effectively lead others, excellent planning, organizational, and communication skills, and the ability to create a culture of achievement at all levels of the organization.

CORE VALUES: Reject Passivity, Accept Responsibility, Lead Courageously, Invest Eternally

Promotion, new job, and change of industries:

Objective	A role in which I am expected to analyze problems and needs, develop and implement creative and profitable solutions, and be accountable and rewarded for the results; willing to travel as is necessary.

Key-word Rich and Customized

When the decision-maker first looks at your résumé, the first thing they'll see will be an **Objective Statement,** key-word rich and customized to the promotion you are seeking.

The first two elements (exact title and two or three position requirements) are self-explanatory.

The third element (your unique contribution to solve their need going unmet) may require an explanation and example.

For your "Unique Contribution," in a few words, you'll identify a critical need they may not know they have, but you know, or believe the company has, that YOU can satisfy when they promote or hire you.

Doing this will help you differentiate yourself from your competition and help catapult you to be the TOP CANDIDATE.

Here's why:

Often companies are blind to their deficiencies and have needs they don't know they have. BUT as a proactive, alert Motivated 10%er© with both your own and your company's interests at heart, surely you can identify, or already have identified, needs they have, or have ideas about how you could cost-effectively improve their bottom line.

A need you see that decision-makers are unaware of is a perfect opportunity for YOU to instantly become the TOP CANDIDATE.

Here's How I Successfully Applied my System

My first job out of grad school was as property human resources director with Marriott Hotels. After two years I was promoted from a 300-employee hotel in Miami to over 1,000 employees in Philadelphia.

Both jobs required me to conduct skills and management training and over five years, I became an enthusiastic and reasonably effective trainer.

After leaving Marriott, my next job was a back-step in title, an increase in pay, and better hours. I became supervisor of plant compensation in a metal cutting plant in upstate New York. I immediately noticed executives and the unions got a lot of attention, but mid-level managers and supervisors were largely ignored.

I had identified a need going unmet.

For about a year, while learning my new job in an unfamiliar environment, I paid attention, asked a lot of questions, built my reputation, and got very clear on a need I saw that was going unmet. I put together a fact-based proposal with observations, rationales, recommendations, timetables, measurable benefits, and costs for the various initiatives I knew with certainty I could effectively implement.

Following the chain of command, I gave my plan to my immediate boss. Because he was one of those bosses who would trash, ignore, or take credit for good ideas that weren't his, I found a valid reason to give a copy of my plan to a peer manager of his (a man of integrity whom I admired. I knew he would value my proposal, and I hoped he would become my boss if senior management accepted it.)

As expected, my boss trashed my proposal, and as I hoped, the peer manager loved it, endorsed it, and forwarded it to the division VP of industrial relations.

The VP told me to create a job description focusing on the needs I had identified (training and development, succession development planning for mid-level managers and supervisors), recruiting, - all the things I loved to do and did well.

Then he promoted me into the job I created, and I got the new boss I wanted.

My initiative brought me to the attention of senior executives in Corporate, which led to, among other things, a six-month posting in Germany to provide industrial relations support to reorganize the European Division, an offer to relocate to Germany as the European Division Director of Industrial Relations (which I declined because I had learned the division would be up for sale), responsibility to staff a new facility in another state, and then a promotion to a larger division in Connecticut, as heir apparent to that division's Director of Industrial Relations.

My INNER GAME initiative led to that six-month assignment in Europe, which in turn led to those opportunities. Then a new company and another promotion, and five years as Latin American Area Director of Human Resources for 13 countries in Central and South America. And from there, working, training and consulting around the US, Europe, Australia, and the Asia-Pacific Rim.

All because my Inner Game gave me the job search self-confidence to present myself as the solution to a need going unmet.

As a reinforcing reminder: Three times over 18 years in Corporate America, I created jobs or promotions for myself by identifying needs going unmet, and then presenting myself as the solution to those needs.

Doing all that made me the hero of my story.

You are poised to become the heroine of your story.

Assignment #8. Custom Objective Statement

Using the examples, create your custom Objective Statement.

On now to the final step - your targeted cover letter to accompany your custom résumé.

CHAPTER 5

Your Targeted Cover Letter & Bringing It All Together

Let me remind you that with **BE THE MEATBALL Top Candidate Custom Résumé System©** *you will only apply where your accomplishments and skills will make you the top candidate.*

Suitability Shortcut© Exercise to See if You Can Be the Top Candidate

Since I'm advising you to only apply for promotions where you can be the TOP CANDIDATE, the *Suitability Shortcut©* will let you quickly determine if your accomplishments and skills will make it worthwhile for you to apply, or not.

Completing this short exercise before you apply will save you immense amounts of time, energy, emotion, and frustration.

You're going to complete the YOU SEEK / I OFFER portion of your targeted cover letter - before you even think about going to the effort of creating a custom résumé.

The first thing you'll do is analyze the specific requirements for the promotion to identify the *four – seven* primary ones.

If you are certain you meet those primary requirements, selectively copy-and-paste them (this guarantees keyword recognition) into the left-hand, YOU SEEK column of your targeted cover letter.

Then do a requirement-by-requirement comparison in the I OFFER column.

Here's what a completed Suitability Shortcut© looked like. Perfect fit!

YOU SEEK	I OFFER
1. "Experience to direct all activities related to the research and development of hardware and software products, including creation, analysis, development, prototyping, testing and successful transition to manufacturing."	More than 15 years of experience leading product development teams in a range of industries — chemical, military, and medical — both domestically and internationally, and success with transitioning designs from R&D to Manufacturing
2. "Manage the development of the division's full line of products, working with domestic and international operational staff"	Proven ability to manage the efforts of a diverse electro-mechanical product line. Strong ability to develop effective, lasting partnerships with all stakeholders with diverse backgrounds
3. "Review, validate, prioritize and allocate resources to manage and resolve problem reports"	Solid track record eliminating production delays without sacrificing quality, market reputation or product integrity while coordinating the work of as many as 12 business-critical projects simultaneously
4. "Develop and implement new policies, processes, procedures, and systems to ensure an efficient and effective product development"	Drive to achieve innovation, measurable reduction in unit production cost and creative solutions to bottom-line problems. A flexible approach to system design utilizing proven techniques
5. "Promote cooperation and communication between the various groups within the division to ensure operational efficiency and division profitability"	High level of commitment by all parties and highly successful projects both domestically and overseas
6. "Communicate performance metrics, evaluate performance, coach and counsel employees. Maintain harmonious employee/employer relationship"	A balanced left/right brain approach to managing employees developed over the years of mentoring from Engineering, HR and Organizational Development executives. Proven ability to challenge other employees to achieve

7. "Promote the Division, its' products, services, and relationships with key and potential customers"	Effective and authentic company testimony to help win new business and maintain current clients

First Example of Custom Cover Letter

Here is Greg's full custom cover letter and résumé. The seven YOU SEEK areas became the seven sub-categories of accomplishments in his résumé.

Dear Ms. Last Name,

Thank you for inviting me to submit my résumé for the position of Director of Engineering by Company's Product Name line. I am very excited, and the more I compare your requirements with my experience and interests, the more excited I become.

I want you to know right up front that I am not a plodding engineer; rather, I am a forward-thinking engineering leader with a proven track record for delivering high-quality products, on time and to standards. I have earned a reputation for innovation, rigorous testing procedures, a proactive and hands-on approach to cost reduction, meeting deadlines on large and small-scale projects, and the ability to lead and develop engineers and technicians on my projects.

Here is how I compare in terms of what you seek for the position and what I offer:

YOU SEEK	I OFFER
1. "Experience to direct all activities related to the research and development of hardware and software products, including creation, analysis, development, prototyping, testing and successful	More than 15 years of experience leading product development teams in a range of industries - chemical, military, and medical - both domestically and internationally, and success with

transition to manufacturing."	transitioning designs from R&D to Manufacturing
2. "Manage the development of the division's full line of products, working with domestic and international operational staff"	Proven ability to manage the efforts of a diverse electro-mechanical product line. Strong ability to develop effective, lasting partnerships with all stakeholders with diverse backgrounds
3. "Review, validate, prioritize and allocate resources to manage and resolve problem reports"	Solid track record eliminating production delays without sacrificing quality, market reputation or product integrity while coordinating the work of as many as 12 business-critical projects simultaneously
4. "Develop and implement new policies, processes, procedures, and systems to ensure an efficient and effective product development"	Drive to achieve innovation, measurable reduction in unit production cost and creative solutions to bottom-line problems. A flexible approach to system design utilizing proven techniques
5. "Promote cooperation and communication between the various	High level of commitment by all parties and highly

groups within the division to ensure operational efficiency and division profitability"	successful projects both domestically and overseas
6. "Communicate performance metrics, evaluate performance, coach and counsel employees. Maintain harmonious employee/employer relationship"	A balanced left/right brain approach to managing employees developed over the years of mentoring from Engineering, HR and Organizational Development executives. Proven ability to challenge other employees to achieve
7. "Promote the Division, its' products, services, and relationships with key and potential customers"	Effective and authentic company testimony to help win new business and maintain current clients

Please look over my professional profile which describes in further detail some examples of the results of the skills and abilities I bring to the table.

I'll check with you on June 1st to see about our next step, unless you contact me first at phone number.

Thank you very much.

Best regards,

Name

Because he was a perfect match, we knew with 100% certainty he would be interviewed. Using Skype, the requirements, his new résumé, and cover letter, we did intense interviewing practice as we waited for the call.

And a good thing too, because we barely had time to complete one round of interview practice before the recruiter called him. And as you know, the CEO demanded to interview him, and he was hired.

Second Example of Custom Cover Letter

The second example cover letter belongs to the wedding accomplishment woman and is a broadcast email to her network.

She sought referrals to people where her network thought there might be a need for someone with her experience.

Although she did not have experience in her new industry, her résumé demonstrated her creativity and her ability to learn. She was interviewed immediately, changed industries, and was hired.

Broadcast Email to Business Network

> Hello All!
>
> I don't generally share news through a blanket email. However, I've given my two weeks' notice to the Club and the chances of me seeing all of you within that time are slim.
>
> A couple of you may already know that I've given notice; however, this email has a request attached to it, so please do read on...
>
> I have worked with the Club for the past six years, have met many great people during that time, and have had some wonderful experiences. Since the acquisition this past January, I've been giving a great deal of thought to my future - where I am and where I want to go. The conclusion I've come to is that I've done my very best here and the time has come to move on. This has been a very difficult decision to make; I'll miss working with and seeing each of you.
>
> Thursday, May 31st will be my final day at the Club.

I do not yet have a new position. Rather, I decided to take a leap of faith in order to conduct a full-out job search on my own time, rather than do a "stealth" search on the Club's time.

My request is in two parts: Would you please take a few minutes and read my attached résumé? If you find me worthy, would you consider forwarding it to folks within your network where you feel there may be a need for someone with my credentials, work ethic, and experience?

I feel really good about this decision and will miss the Club. However, I believe if I never risk, I can never gain, and I am looking forward to the future with giddy excitement.

Please know that I consider my request as a debt owed from one professional to another, and if I can repay your kindness, you have but to ask.

I hope not to lose touch. Please call on me if I can be of assistance to you. My personal contact information is - email address and my cell is ###.###.####.

Thank you for so many great memories.

Email signature block

Her network was impressed with her courage to leave without having a new job, and with her integrity to not conduct a job search on her employer's time. They felt the authenticity of her words. In no time flat, she had referrals that led to a new career. She has since survived two restructurings and received two promotions.

Here is a link to her broadcast referral cover letter and résumé: https://topcandidateresumes.com/resumes/jen.

Your Targeted Cover Letter

When you completed your Suitability Shortcut©, you prepared the essence of the cover letter, so finishing it off will be a piece of cake.

Greg's cover letter stopped the CEO dead in his tracks and led him right into the résumé, so I recommend you follow that model. Avoid platitudes and "buttering-them-up air words," like *"Yours is a wonderful company and I would be honored to blah blah blah."*

Use keywords from the requirements for the YOU SEEK column and be as succinct as possible in your I OFFER parallel assessment.

If you can keep your cover letter to one page, so much the better. But don't force it. Greg's was two pages and it did not hurt him. As you close the letter, make sure you state an action step - what you would like the reader to do.

Assignment #9: Your Targeted Cover Letter

Taking guidance from the examples on the website, please write your targeted cover letter for the promotion you seek.

Your Custom Résumé

Time now to create your TOP CANDIDATE custom résumé to win interviews for the next promotion you seek.

Presented in the order you'll use them, you'll need these items:

1. Promotion Requirements
2. Suitability Shortcut©
3. Text Column©
4. Custom Objective Statement
5. Table of six Skills that support your accomplishment statements
6. Accomplishment statements matching the promotion requirements
7. Final Personal Accomplishment statement converted into Professional Accomplishment statement
8. Part B
9. Completed targeted cover letter

Once you've gathered them, do these two things:

First, using the promotion requirements and your Suitability Shortcut©, make certain the accomplishments and skills you have decided to use are significant and match the promotion's requirements.

If they don't, check your Accomplishments Data Bank to see if you have any that could be edited to fit.

If not, I recommend you save your energy and your Inner Game. Skip this promotion, and don't apply until you've found an opportunity where you're positive your accomplishments and skills will make you the TOP CANDIDATE.

Second, if you're going ahead, proof-read everything you prepare. Have someone else read your résumé and cover letter. Ask them to look for mistakes, typos, inconsistencies, or anything else that just looks or sounds funny.

Pick Your Layout of Your New Résumé

If you're ready to proceed, the first thing to do is decide on the layout of your new résumé.

The first half of your résumé will focus on your relevant skills and accomplishments, not your job history.

You've seen several formats on my website. To create your first set of custom documents, I suggest you use Greg Pease's "disruptive" résumé and cover letter as your model.

Page 1 of your résumé will include your Text Column©, custom Objective Statement, table of Special Skills and Abilities, and the start of your Representative Professional Accomplishments.

After your personal contact data at the top of the résumé, the first text box is the **Text Column© on the left side of Page 1**. This will contain the highlights of what you bring to the *"World of Work."* As you saw in the résumés of Alejandro and Gary, it does not need to run the full length of the page.

The next text box is your **Custom Objective Statement**. Referring to the promotion requirements, make sure you have selected two, three or four critical requirements that you meet, then add a final one — a problem or need you're certain they have but that they don't know they have —for which you are the solution. The fewer words, the better.

Then, the **Special Skills and Abilities table**. I recommend a table of your six most relevant skills. Use keywords from the promotion posting and make certain they support your accomplishment statements in the next section.

Next, your Representative Professional Accomplishments

Organize them into subcategories based on the order of the YOU SEEK items in your Suitability Shortcut.©

The keywords you select from the requirements and your Suitability Shortcut© will become the subcategory headings for this section of your résumé.

The first subcategory should be your most professionally significant and the most relevant to the promotion. The first accomplishment statement in support of it should be your most impressive accomplishment.

Note: Without changing the essence or results of an accomplishment, I will sometimes make gentle edits in the focus/content of an accomplishment statement if I want it to fit under a specific subcategory heading.

Caution: Make sure you can substantiate anything and everything you put in your résumé and cover letter. It's all fair game during the interviews.

It's OK if your Representative Professional Accomplishment statements fill Page 2 or may even continue onto Page 3.

I have found that decision-makers will read as many pages as there are in a résumé, **so long as the information is** R-E-L-E-V-A-N-T.

And the best way to make it relevant is to customize your credentials.

You must keep that in mind.

Final Personal Accomplishment Statement Converted into Professional Accomplishment Statement.

On Greg's résumé, you'll see that he included his personal accomplishment under the heading *"In my spare time."*

Alejandro chose to position his statement in a modified oval at the bottom of his final page, where it would be impossible to miss.

Rachel's is the final accomplishment statement, just before her Part B.

And Jennifer, because she used a format that did not have a Part B, ended her résumé with her statement. Positioning it there was very effective because it was the last thing decision-makers read about her.

However, you choose to do it, the strategy is to use a strong final accomplishment that will make you a *"memorable Meatball,"* someone decision-makers are looking forward to meeting.

Final Activity

Time to go get the interview.

Please complete your custom résumé and your targeted cover letter.

When both are ready for submission, give them one final proof reading, take a deep breath, congratulate yourself, and send your packet off.

Share the moment with your family and think about your heroic journey from losing to **winning your Inner Game**, from Generic 90%er to **Motivated 10%er.**

Congratulations! You're on your way.

And before you put things away, please continue to the end of the book.

Final Assignment: Your Transformation to Motivated 10%er

As you completed the Inner Game portion of the course and began creating your LIFETIME CAREER PLAN©, I asked you to reflect on the progress of your transformation to Motivated 10%er© and told you you'd see those questions again.

Here they are. Please take a few minutes to reflect in writing on all you've learned, realized, felt and experienced from when you started to now.

1. Emotional and/or attitudinal transformations?
2. Big Ah-Ha's, maybe around being a Victim, or no longer a Victim?
3. Changes in attitude you have made and are committed to making?
4. Thoughts about the Boilerplate Herd, Generic 90%ers© and Motivated 10%ers©?
5. Your INNER GAME now vs. when you started the course?
6. Your job search self-confidence?
7. Anything else?

My Last Bit of Advice

As a Motivated 10%er© for the rest of your career:

- Keep your Accomplishments and Skills Data Banks current. Be alert so you recognize accomplishments as you achieve them.
- False modesty and *"Aw shucks. I was just doin' my job"* is not Motivated 10%er behavior.

- Allow yourself to take credit for your accomplishments and do what you've learned to do: *Follow the System.*
- Periodically review your LIFETIME CAREER PLAN©. Keep your current PLAN as your foundation and modify as needed. It will be your blueprint to win your Inner Game and maintain your TOP CANDIDATE mindset for the rest of your career.

In Closing: Your Transformation From "Passed Over" To "Promoted" & Possible Next Steps

The day I completed the final draft of this book, I received a LinkedIn message from a woman asking if several years ago I had given a series of free résumé workshops north of Seattle in the town where I used to live? I had, and she told me what she learned in my workshop was the reason she quickly won interviews for her last two jobs.

She said she has never forgotten that I closed my workshop with these words:

You are SO much more than your 'dates-and-duties' spaghetti résumé."

They were meaningful to her, and I hope they are to you as well.

Now that you know how to win interviews as a TOP CANDIDATE whenever you want them, if you'd like to take your job search self-confidence to the next level with me to **increase your interview self-confidence,** here are two additional courses I offer:

<u>ROCK-SOLID SELF-CONFIDENCE IN TEAM INTERVIEWS</u>© - In a cohort of no more than six, over three months, you'll acquire team interviewing skills using your new custom credentials and the requirements for promotions. You'll learn to be confidentially brilliant in TEAM INTERVIEWS.

CUSTOM 1:1 TOP CANDIDATE INTERVIEWING PRACTICE© - For three months, for as many one-to-one phone or web-based sessions as you need, we will use your new custom credentials and the requirements of as many promotional or new job opportunities as you wish to practice 1:1 interviewing and develop rock-solid interview self-confidence.

You'll find links to these two courses here: https://topcandidateresumes.com/courses.

And if you are interested in all of my DIY custom résumé books . . .

- How to Win Your Inner Game! Update Your Attitude before You 'Update Your Résumé'
- How to Get Interviews! Stop Sending Job Search Junk Mail
- Burn Your Résumé! You Need a Professional Profile
- Kindle "O" is for "Objective" - 4 Steps to Be the Ideal Candidate
- Kindle "A" is for "Accomplishment" - 7 Steps to Stop Minimizing Yourself
- Kindle "S" is for "Skills" - 3 Steps to Tastefully Boast and Be Memorable

And finally, if you wish to contact me, please email me at Hello@topcandidateresumes.com

Best regards,
Don // topcandidateresumes.com

Postscript

November 19, 2019

When you read the **Success Stories** on my site, you read Navy vet Gary Baguio's résumé – the one with pictures of jet fighters he was responsible for, his seven rows of Navy commendation ribbons, and his story.

Last night, as I finished editing the proof for this book, I received an email from Gary containing this YouTube video, photo, and testimonial.

> *"The most important achievement I gained by working with Don was both professional and personal. I gained my self-confidence back by re-joining the workforce all because of my resume Don prepared for me. Without him, I would still be applying for jobs with no interviews."* Gary Baguio

I believe in synchronicity, and so am sharing it with you.

Thank you, Gary. https://bit.ly/3ceKuKV

Don -

www.ingramcontent.com/pod-product-compliance
Lightning Source LLC
Chambersburg PA
CBHW030957090426
42737CB00007B/569

* 9 7 8 0 5 7 8 6 0 8 8 1 5 *